CONTENTS

FIGURES

TABLES

PANELS

CASE STUDIES

AUTHORS

GERALDINE GRADY (Dip. in HRM, MBS IR & HRM, Dip. in Business & Personal Coaching, MCIPD) has worked as the WLB Research Project Manager on the *2007 Work-Life Balance in Ireland* study at the Centre for Innovation & Structural Change (CISC) at the National University of Ireland, Galway. She works as a consultant to many private and public sector organisations and lectures at the Galway-Mayo Institute of Technology (GMIT) in the areas of human resource management, organisational behaviour, and human resource development. Her research interest is work-life balance and she has presented her work at national and international conferences. Prior to this, Geraldine worked for almost 20 years in human resource management for multi-national organisations in the West of Ireland. Her most recent publication in the *Journal of Managerial Psychology* in the area of work-life balance is entitled 'Work-life integration: Experiences of mid-career professional working mothers'. She is a member of the Chartered Institute of Personnel & Development (CIPD) and the Irish Coach Institute.

ALMA McCARTHY (Dip. Training & Education, BBS with French, MCIPD, PhD) is a Lecturer in Management at the National University of Ireland, Galway and Research Director of the *2007 Work-Life Balance in Ireland* study at the Centre for Innovation & Structural Change, National University of Ireland, Galway. She lectures in the areas of human resource management, organisational behaviour, and human resource development. Her research interests include performance management, employee training and development, work-life balance, and multi-rater (360°) feedback systems. Alma's publications include articles in journals such as the *Personnel Review, Advances in Developing Human Resources, Journal of European Industrial Training*, the *International Journal of Manpower Studies*, and the *Journal of Vocational Educational Training*; papers at national and international conferences, including the Irish Academy of Management, the European Academy of Management and the American Society for Industrial & Organizational Psychology; and numerous co-authored chapters in edited books. She is a member of the Chartered Institute of Personnel & Development (CIPD), the American Academy of Management (AoM), the Society for Industrial & Organisational Psychology (SIOP), and currently serves on the national council of the Irish Academy of Management (IAM) as Vice-Chair.

COLETTE DARCY (BBS, MBS in HRM, PhD) is a Lecturer in Human Resource Management at the National College of Ireland. She is currently programme director for the MA in HRM at the National College of Ireland, in addition to lecturing on numerous undergraduate and postgraduate programmes in the area of human resource management. Colette recently was awarded the EMF / Emerald Outstanding Doctoral Thesis  Award for her research examining employee fairness perceptions and claiming behaviour. Her research interests also extend to organisational justice, work-life balance and the changing nature of employment and she has presented her work at national and international conferences, including the Irish Academy of Management, the International HRM Conference and the European Academy of Management. Prior to returning to academia, Colette worked for a number of years in management consultancy, specialising in reward strategies and change management.

MELRONA KIRRANE (BA(Psych), BA in HRM, PhD) is a Chartered Occupational Psychologist and Fellow of the Chartered Institute of Personnel & Development. Awarded her doctorate in Organisational Psychology by Queen's University, Belfast in 1992, she has worked in Dublin City University Business School as lecturer in Organisational  Psychology for the last nine years. She is the Academic Director of the Master of Business Administration at DCUBS and teaches on a range of advanced management programmes. Melrona's key areas of expertise include leadership, organisational diagnosis, managing change, employee motivation and personnel selection. She has been visiting lecturer at Northeastern University, Boston and Lancaster University Management School, and is an external examiner for the University of Ulster. Along with book chapters and scholarly publications in both national and international conferences and journals, such as the *Journal of Managerial Psychology, Equal Opportunities International, The Irish Journal of Applied Social Studies* and *The Irish Journal of Psychology,* her current research projects focus on management learning and development, workaholism and work-life balance, managing change, individual leadership and organisational silence. Melrona regularly consults to the professional and financial services industries in the areas of talent management, leadership and managing change.

Acknowledgements

This guide represents a culmination of extensive research resulting in the *2007 Work-Life Balance in Ireland* study, which gathered work-life balance data from HR managers / directors, middle / line managers and employees.

Accordingly, the authors would like to acknowledge and express their appreciation to a number of people and organisations who provided assistance and support in bringing it to fruition:

- The Centre for Innovation & Structural Change (CISC) and the National University of Ireland, Galway for their support during the research project.
- The Irish Research Council for the Humanities & Social Sciences (IRCHSS) for providing financial support to carry out the empirical research.
- The HR directors / managers, middle / line managers and employees in the private and public sector organisations, who participated in the study: Accenture; Boston Scientific; Chanelle Pharmaceuticals; Dell; Department of Enterprise, Trade & Employment; Department of Justice, Equality & Law Reform; Department of Social & Family Affairs; ESB; Galway University Hospitals; GlaxoSmithKline; HP; Intel; Medtronic and the Revenue Commissioners.
- A special word of thanks to Michael Loughnane, ESB; Jacqueline McGrath, Intel; Dorothy Kelly, Medtronic; Martina Colville, Department of Justice, Equality & Law Reform; and Michelle Carroll, Revenue Commissioners.
- The employees who provided their own personal real-life case studies to support the evidence presented on work-life balance at the different life-cycle stages.
- Prof. Jan Cleveland, Pennsylvania State University, for her assistance and guidance throughout the project.
- Brendan McGinty, Director of Industrial Relations & Human Resource Services, IBEC, for contributing the *Foreword* and endorsing this guide.
- Mary Connaughton, Head of HR Development, IBEC, for her valuable contribution to this guide.
- Brian O'Kane and Oak Tree Press for publishing this guide.

FOREWORD

In today's competitive environment, employers continually are seeking ways to manage and retain key talent in the organisation, as well as to attract prospective employees. Employees are more conscious of achieving the right balance between their work and other aspects of their lives.

Work-Life Balance: Policies & Initiatives in Irish Organisations provides a thorough and accessible review of key research on work-life balance (WLB) in Irish organisations and builds the business case for investment in such initiatives. It sets out a comprehensive framework for designing, implementing and evaluating WLB initiatives, thus providing a valuable tool for managers and organisations.

The guide draws on the *2007 Work-Life Balance in Ireland* study, carried out at the Centre for Innovation & Structural Change at NUI Galway. This research showed that there are a variety of WLB policies and initiatives currently implemented in Irish organisations, but that many adopt an informal, as opposed to a systematic and planned, approach. It also found that supportive initiatives (such as on-site medical facilities and memberships) are more common in the private sector as compared to reduced working hours and flexi-time arrangements, which are more widespread in the public sector.

Implementing WLB policies and initiatives needs to be aligned strategically to the overall company mission and goals and a systematic and planned approach is best. Increased involvement by middle / line managers in the formulation of policies is essential, as they can act as the critical link to successful implementation of such policies. Employers and employees must work together to find the right strategy to meet the needs of the business and to support employees in managing work-life balance.

Given the increasing debate on work-life balance, both nationally and internationally, together with the realisation that employees are the real source of competitive advantage for organisations, this guide is both timely and opportune. IBEC is pleased to be associated with it and believes that this practical "how to" guide will benefit and support all organisations of whatever size to address work-life balance issues in a fair, equitable and sustainable manner.

Brendan McGinty
Director – Industrial Relations & Human Resource Services
IBEC

1: INTRODUCTION

"One of the clearest findings emerging from much of this [widespread work-life balance] research is that, despite the wide range of policies supporting family-friendly and more flexible working, many are still not meeting the needs of employees, not achieving their full potential, or providing value for the organisations that have introduced them."
— Work-Life Balance Network (2004: 4)

Thus quotation from the Work-Life Balance Network, a scheme set up under the EU-funded EQUAL Community Initiative, accurately depicts the state of work-life balance policy and practice in Irish organisations today.

The purpose of this book is to provide managers and organisations with a guide to design, deliver, manage, and evaluate work-life balance policies and programmes effectively and successfully at enterprise level.

This chapter presents the book's objectives, as well as describing the 2007 Work-Life Balance in Ireland *study that informs much of the book.*

The meaning of work-life balance for employees and organisations is discussed. A holistic model is presented to enable organisations to design, implement and evaluate work-life balance initiatives, policies and practices. This model is used subsequently to organise the book.

Driving the Work-Life Balance Agenda

The reconciliation of work and personal life has become increasingly important in recent years across the European Union.[1] Work-life balance has come to the fore in contemporary human resource management debates, because the increasing, and sometimes excessive, demands of work in developed societies are perceived to present a distinctive problem that needs to be addressed.[2] The implications of conflicting work and family responsibilities for people management and work structures are wide-ranging. These issues not only operate at policy level, but work-life balance, family-friendly work practices, employee-friendliness, and flexible working arrangements are contemporary work-related practices that have a significant impact on social partnership, people management, and policy-making, both nationally and at EU level.

The recent *Future of HR in Europe* report[3] draws on data gathered from 1,355 HR executives across 27 countries. It identifies the management of work-life balance as one of the top three challenges facing HR through to 2015. The Irish HR executive respondents ranked work-life balance as the second most important challenge after talent management. It is timely, therefore, that we examine what organisations can, and should, do to manage work-life balance initiatives successfully. This book aims to act as a key resource in this regard.

Objectives of this Book

The purpose of this book is to present a guide for managers and organisations considering new work-life balance, or flexible working, policies and programmes or revising existing ones. The book will assist in the design, implementation, management and monitoring of work-life balance in organisations.

By incorporating the findings from the *2007 Work-Life Balance in Ireland* study (see **page 4**), and by presenting examples of work-life balance policies and practices in Irish private and public sector organisations, this book also aims to:

- Establish the business case for work-life balance.

- Provide a practical hands-on, step-by-step guide to enable organisations to adopt and implement appropriate WLB strategies to match the culture and business needs of their organisation.

- Provide a comprehensive approach to managing and implementing work-life balance initiatives, drawing on the perspectives, views, and issues relevant at multiple levels within the organisation – for example, senior management, middle management, and employees.

---

[1]   European Foundation for the Improvement of Living & Working Conditions (2002).
[2]   Guest (2001).
[3]   Boston Consulting Group and the European Association for Personnel Management (2007).

What is Meant by Work-Life Balance?

Work-Life Balance: The Employee Perspective

Work-life balance (WLB) refers to the sense of balance and satisfaction employees experience between their work / professional and personal lives. When the demands of work and life exist in harmony with each other, then work-life balance is achieved. WLB is built on a belief that, while work is important to each individual, and to society as a whole, achievement and enjoyment in everyday life beyond the workplace are also essential to human and societal well-being.[4] Thus, work-life balance is concerned with how employees manage and maintain a satisfactory balance between work and personal time and responsibilities.

WLB is also used to refer to family-friendly policies and practices. Family-friendly working arrangements involve measures to support, or assist, employees in managing the dual responsibilities of work and family life. However, WLB is a more inclusive concept, as it is concerned not only with work and family domains – WLB refers to the various personal life domains, including family, community, recreation and personal time. In this book, the term 'work-life balance' is used in its broadest sense to capture all the aspects of an employee's personal and work life.

Work-Life Balance: The Organisational Perspective

From an organisational perspective, WLB arrangements and practices refer to initiatives voluntarily introduced by firms that facilitate the reconciliation of employees' work and personal lives. Such initiatives include:

- **Temporal arrangements** that allow employees to reduce the number of hours they work (for example, job-sharing / work-sharing, part-time working and term-time working).

- **Flexible working arrangements**, such as flexi-time, time off in lieu, tele-working / home-working / e-working.

- **Work-life balance supports**, such as employee counselling, tuition / education fee support, on-site or discounted medical facilities, and the provision of financial advisers.

- **Childcare** facilities on-site or financial support for childcare off-site (for example, through subsidised childcare).

As well as the discretionary work-life balance policies and practices that organisations operate, there are also many statutory provisions geared towards work-life balance that organisations must offer (see **Chapter 2**).

---

[4]   Joshi *et al.* (2002).

The *2007 Work-Life Balance in Ireland* Study

A study on work-life balance in Ireland was undertaken at the National University of Ireland, Galway in collaboration with the National College of Ireland, Dublin City University Business School and Penn State University in the USA. The study was funded by the Irish Research Council for the Humanities & Social Sciences (IRCHSS) and the research was carried out in both the private and public sectors. A number of organisations were contacted to establish their willingness to participate in the study from March to July 2007.

The objectives of the study were:

- To develop a holistic, multi-perspective model of work-life balance perceptions, antecedents, and consequences.

- To identify the outcomes of work-life balance and imbalance at an individual, organisational, and social level.

- To compare manager and employee perceptions of work-life balance provisions and arrangements.

- To develop a set of recommendations for organisations and policy-makers, aimed at reconciling more effectively the conflicting demands between work and non-working life.

Fifteen large organisations participated in the study – 10 from the private sector and five from the public sector. A three-strand approach was used to gather the data at multiple levels in each organisation:

- A sample of employees from each organisation was chosen to participate in the study and a questionnaire (electronic or paper-based) was sent to them.

- Telephone or face-to-face interviews were conducted with a sample of middle / line managers in each participating organisation.

- A face-to-face interview was conducted with the HR director / manager.

In total, 729 employees completed and returned usable responses from the 1,300 questionnaires distributed (representing a 56% response rate). In the 15 organisations, 133 middle / line managers and 15 HR directors / managers were interviewed.

This book draws on the findings from the *2007 Work-Life Balance in Ireland* study,[5] which provide a useful and informative foundation from which the best practice WLB model presented in this book is developed. The inclusion of data from three stakeholder groups – HR directors / managers, middle / line managers, and employees – is particularly useful in informing best practice work-life balance policies and programmes.

---

[5]   McCarthy *et al.* (2008).

Book Content & Structure

This book is organised around an eight-step model for designing, implementing, monitoring and evaluating work-life balance practices (see **Figure 1.1**).

Figure 1.1: An Eight-Step Model of Work-Life Balance Design, Implementation & Evaluation

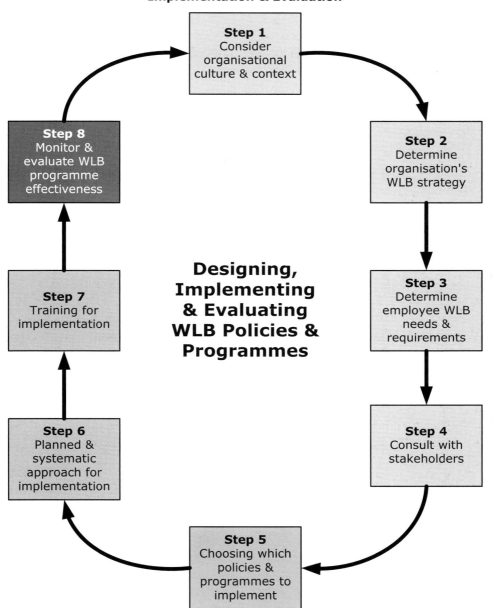

Chapter 2 reviews the factors that have contributed to the rise of work-life balance at a societal, organisational and individual level. The chapter also examines the business case for WLB and explores government action in relation to increasing awareness and promotion of WLB, including the relevant statutory instruments.

Chapter 3 sets out the issues of importance when designing work-life balance policies and programmes and discusses steps 1 to 4 of the model.

Chapter 4 presents the critical success factors in implementing work-life balance policies and practices (steps 5 to 7 of the model), while **Chapter 5** sets out how to evaluate and monitor work-life balance programmes in operation (step 8), to ensure their effectiveness for the organisation and its employees.

Chapter 6 examines the reported benefits and challenges of operating WLB programmes and initiatives from an employee and organisational perspective and identifies management and organisational strategies to address such challenges.

Chapter 7 briefly reviews the key WLB issues raised in this book and explores the future of WLB by looking at developments nationally and at an EU level.

2: THE RISE OF WORK-LIFE BALANCE

"The most important contribution of management in the 20th century was the fifty-fold increase in the productivity of the manual worker in manufacturing. The most important contribution management needs to make in the 21st century is similarly to increase productivity of the knowledge worker."
– Peter Drucker

While some commentators are quick to dismiss work-life balance as the latest fad in a long line of trendy management quick-fixes, the reality is that a number of societal, organisational and individual changes over the past two decades have combined to create a momentum for work-life balance policies, initiatives and programmes. This chapter seeks to identify these factors and, in doing so, provides the contextual background that has brought us to the point where work-life balance is not only a central issue for individuals and organisations, but also for society.

We begin the chapter by asking what are the factors that have contributed to the rise of work-life balance at a societal, organisational and individual level. Looking at these factors, we ask how the changing social and economic context has impacted on our working lives and how this is likely to manifest itself going forward. Why are organisations interested in work-life balance initiatives and what is the underlying business case for moving WLB onto the strategic board agenda? What are the perceived barriers to the introduction of WLB initiatives from an organisational perspective? What factors influence individual employees to engage, or crucially not to engage, in such initiatives? Finally, we look at what government is doing in increasing awareness and promotion of WLB, including the various statutory instruments relevant to the area. The answers to these questions dispel attempts to dismiss work-life balance as a fad; rather, they force us to recognise its importance both today and, more importantly, its likely pivotal role in the workplace of tomorrow.

The factors combining to create the recent pressure for the introduction of work-life balance policies, practices and initiatives can be divided into three broad categories:

- External / societal factors.
- Internal / organisational factors.
- Individual factors.

These three groupings (see **Figure 2.1**) increasingly are creating pressure for the introduction of workplace arrangements that help workers to achieve a more satisfactory work-life balance and so are discussed in this chapter.

Figure 2.1: Factors Combining to Create Pressure for the Introduction of Work-Life Balance Policies, Practices & Initiatives

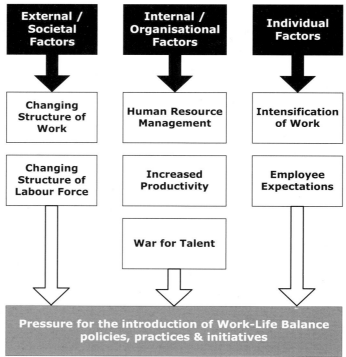

External Societal Factors

The Changing Structure of Work

Work activity has changed radically over the past decade. The number of traditional manufacturing and agriculture-related jobs has fallen dramatically and in their place we have witnessed an unprecedented rise in the number of service-related positions. **Table 2.1** demonstrates this point, with 136,000 individuals employed in the agricultural sector in the period March to May 1998, compared to 114,700 in the same period in 2007. This decrease is mirrored by an increase in the number of individuals working in the services sector over the same period, from 929,600 in 1998 to over 1.4 million by 2007. What is also notable about this shift is the rise in the number of women entering the workforce: 593,400 in 1998, rising to 899,500 by May 2007. Unsurprisingly, the largest growth sector for employment of women was within the services sector.

Table 2.1: Persons aged 15 & Over in Employment (ILO), Classified by Sex & Broad NACE Economic Sector ('000s)

Broad economic sector	March - May 1998	March - May 1999	March - May 2000	March - May 2001	March - May 2002	March - May 2003	March - May 2004	March - May 2005	March - May 2006	March - May 2007
Males										
Agriculture	120.0	121.6	118.1	109.2	111.4	102.9	105.8	102.6	103.8	103.1
Industry	331.1	350.9	371.9	394.8	388.1	399.2	404.5	436.1	454.0	475.6
Services	449.6	475.6	502.6	515.0	528.3	538.9	554.8	571.3	604.2	617.2
Females										
Agriculture	16.0	15.7	14.8	13.3	12.7	13.7	11.1	11.1	10.7	11.6
Industry	97.3	98.9	103.8	103.3	99.2	98.3	102.1	100.5	97.2	96.2
Services	480.1	526.4	560.2	586.3	624.3	640.4	657.8	707.6	747.0	791.7
All persons										
Agriculture	136.0	137.3	132.9	122.5	124.0	116.6	117.0	113.7	114.5	114.7
Industry	428.4	449.8	475.7	498.1	487.2	497.5	506.5	536.6	551.2	571.8
Services	929.6	1,002.0	1,062.8	1,101.3	1,152.6	1,179.3	1,212.7	1,278.9	1,351.2	1,408.9
Total persons	**1,494.0**	**1,589.1**	**1,671.4**	**1,721.9**	**1,763.9**	**1,793.4**	**1,836.2**	**1,929.2**	**2,017.0**	**2,095.4**

Source: CSO – Quarterly National Household Survey.

The shift away from what is generally considered unskilled to skilled workers is a significant feature of a changing economy.[6] The change reflects both the requirement for new skills to meet the emerging jobs created in the new economy and also the rising skills demand of existing roles. This rise in skills can be seen in the number of individual employees who categorise themselves either as managers or professionals. From the figures released by the Central Statistics Office (CSO) for the period March-May 1998 to the same period in 2006, there has been a near 10% increase in the managers category and a 60% rise in the professional category (see **Table 2.2**).

The change in the structure of employment is not unique to Ireland. There is an ongoing shift away from jobs in agriculture and industry towards jobs in the services sector across the European Union.[7] In addition, there has been a notable growth in the number of fixed-term contract workers, as well as a rise in part-time employees (albeit among female participants) and temporary workers. It is predicted that female employment will continue to grow over the coming years by as much as 35%,[8] which represents a rate of expansion more than double that forecast for men. These workers represent a new type of worker who tend to choose to work in atypical ways and to use technological advances to their advantage. Thus, these changes have implications for how work and working time is structured in organisations and, in many cases, calls for more family-friendly and flexible working arrangements to be provided by the organisation.

---

[6]   Duggan *et al.* (1997).

[7]   Bodin & Verborgh (2002).

[8]   Sexton *et al.* (2002).

Table 2.2: Persons in Employment (ILO), Classified by Occupation ('000s)

Broad Occupational Group	March - May 1998	March - May 1999	March - May 2000	March - May 2001	March - May 2002	March - May 2003	March - May 2004	March - May 2005	March - May 2006
1. Managers & administrators	284.6	294.3	303.6	309.7	314.1	316.9	319.2	316.7	313.0
2. Professional	147.2	158.5	166.4	173.2	189.5	200.8	211.4	218.6	236.1
3. Associate professional & technical	119.5	130.4	138.6	148.2	155.6	164.9	167.1	171.5	171.1
4. Clerical & secretarial	183.7	199.5	204.3	212.4	224.7	216.9	220.7	236.3	248.0
5. Craft & related	200.4	218.6	227.5	233.5	225.4	242.1	243.6	271.9	286.3
6. Personal & protective service	140.1	152.6	165.5	164.6	168.6	183.6	185.4	198.4	218.2
7. Sales	115.5	126.5	135.9	141.4	144.3	146.2	152.3	164.4	178.4
8. Plant & machine operatives	159.8	162.0	180.3	192.9	184.8	173.7	159.4	167.7	167.7
9. Other	143.3	146.6	149.2	146.1	156.9	148.3	177.0	183.7	198.1
Total persons	**1,494.0**	**1,589.1**	**1,671.4**	**1,721.9**	**1,763.9**	**1,793.4**	**1,836.2**	**1,929.2**	**2,017.0**

Source: CSO – Quarterly National Household Survey.

The Changing Structure of the Labour Force

The structure of the labour market in Ireland has changed dramatically over the last number of years and is likely to continue to do so for the foreseeable future. One of the most notable characteristics of this change has been the increase in the number of women entering and, more importantly, remaining in the workplace. According to CSO figures (June-August 2007), 53.1% of Irish married females are actively engaged in paid employment. It is easy to forget that, until 1973, the 'marriage bar' was still in existence within the Irish labour market, under which married women were prohibited from undertaking certain working roles upon marriage.

Table 2.3 shows the rate of female participation in the workforce by age and marital status. The most notable trend is the significant increase in married women in the workforce. There is also evidence from these figures that women are returning to work later in their lives, possibly after taking time out to raise children. We can see that the number of females aged 45-54 dramatically increased from 46,100 in 1998 to 66,900 by 2007. This trend is reflected across all the older age categories.

Table 2.3: Female Participation in the Workforce, by Age & Marital Status for Quarter 3, 1998 and Quarter 3, 2007 ('000s)

Quarter 3, 1998 Age	15-19	20-24	25-34	35-44	45-54	55-59	60-64	65+	Total
Single	32.4	78.7	85.9	80.3	68.9	49.7	25.2	5.3	60.0
Married	*	56.6	64.1	55.9	42.7	27.3	15.1	3.2	43.0
Separated or divorced	*	*	59.5	61.2	55.6	42.4	23.4	*	53.5
Widowed	*	*	39.9	50.7	48.9	24.1	16.9	2.1	8.6
Total females	**32.5**	**77.7**	**73.8**	**59.4**	**46.1**	**29.5**	**16.7**	**3.0**	**45.9**

Quarter 3, 2007 Age	15-19	20-24	25-34	35-44	45-54	55-59	60-64	65+	Total
Single	33.3	76.6	83.7	77.0	74.5	56.5	38.5	3.9	66.1
Married	*	58.6	71.5	66.5	64.8	45.8	30.0	5.1	53.1
Separated or divorced	*	*	56.0	68.9	72.6	50.8	39.3	8.9	60.6
Widowed	*	*	84.5	74.2	69.1	51.5	29.4	2.5	12.1
Total females	**33.3**	**76.0**	**78.9**	**68.9**	**66.9**	**47.6**	**31.2**	**3.9**	**55.1**

Source: CSO – Quarterly National Household Survey.

The integration of women into the labour force is a trend replicated at a European level also, and has been identified as leading to the intensification of conflict between work and family in the lives of many individuals. The movement from traditional female roles of stay-at-home mother / carer to dual-earner families (where both partners engage in paid employment) has been revolutionary. This has radically changed the way we conceive work and working schedules, gender roles and relationships, and the distribution of domestic and educational tasks in families.[9] Organisations have become increasingly aware that these women are a source of skilled labour and are looking for ways to attract and accommodate the needs of this group.

A second and less discussed change that is occurring within the structure of the labour force is the fact that it is aging. Ireland, again, is not alone in its 'greying' workforce profile, which raises serious questions regarding the future organisation of work and the types of people who are employed. It is likely that we will see calls for greater flexibility in recruiting older workers and greater consideration given to their working arrangements. At a time when more and more older workers are seeking to retire early, it is imperative from a societal perspective that we find new ways of encouraging this greying workforce to stay actively working to ensure adequate labour supply. Older workers could be accommodated to remain in the workforce for longer by providing more flexible working options and arrangements such as reduced working hours.

---

[9]   Poelmans (2003).

Internal Organisational Factors

Human Resource Management

The development of human resource management approaches to managing staff has been critical to a shift in organisational attitudes away from viewing employees as a cost to be borne by the business towards viewing them as a valuable asset of the organisation that is not easily or readily imitated. More recently, employees are being viewed as a business investment with differential needs and interests in work. This development has occurred in response to the external pressures with which organisations have found themselves confronted. It has had the direct effect of allowing organisations to develop a clear focus on the issue of WLB as an approach that may help, through the wider HR agenda, to address some of these issues.

Increased Productivity

In an ever-increasingly competitive business environment, organisations are constantly seeking new ways of achieving increased productivity. The market place is now truly global and, with that, comes competition from all corners of the world. Organisations need to ensure that they are extremely flexible and dynamic if they wish to survive in this marketplace, and so there is a constant and sustained drive to increase productivity and reduce costs. The ability of organisations to motivate their staff to work smarter is seen as one of the key challenges of achieving this increased productivity.

Work-life balance initiatives are viewed as just one way in which organisations can seek to improve or increase the productivity of their workers. For example, studies have found that employees who work from home report significantly higher productivity levels.[10]

The 'War for Talent'

The tight labour market and the need to attract and retain high calibre employees has led firms to strive to be seen as an 'employer of choice' and to adopt best practice HRM policies in order to achieve this. The 'war for talent' is far from over. Indeed, it is likely to increase in importance and intensity, as organisations fight for high-performing star employees on a global scale. Thus, the pressures emanating from within organisations, as well as those at a societal level, are acting as the driving force behind the introduction of work-life balance initiatives.

Individual Factors

The Intensification of Work

The world of work has unquestionably changed. The information worker in today's knowledge economy increasingly is required to be available on a 24-hour, seven days a week (24 / 7) basis. While average working hours are falling in Ireland and across the EU, there is no escaping the fact that work is being carried out at a faster pace.[11] The 'intensification of work' has been found to affect all sectors of industry and all occupational categories. The reasons offered for this rise have been linked to changes in the way work is organised and structured but also have been linked to increased competitive pressures being passed onto workers and the shortening of the official working day. There is increasing evidence to suggest that the type of work carried out is also becoming more complex.[12]

---

[10]   Johnson (1995).
[11]   Boisard *et al.* (2003).
[12]   Green (2004).

The 'always on, always connected' generation is no longer able simply to switch off as they leave the office. Advances in technology such as high-speed broadband, wireless access, personal digital assistants and mobile phones all have transformed our ability to work wherever we find ourselves. The historical link between work and the office as a place of work has been eroded. Employees increasingly find themselves being contacted outside hours or completing work tasks in their personal time.

According to a recent survey by the Irish Forum on the Workplace of the Future, 21% of employees always come home from work too exhausted to engage in other activities.[13] According to recent CIPD survey findings, three out of four people say they are working very hard, with many stating that they are working as hard as they can and could not imagine being able to work harder. The CIPD survey also shows that one in five individuals reported taking work home almost every day, after their official working day has ended. One in three partners of people who work in excess of 48 hours per week felt that this had a negative impact on their personal relationships.[14]

Inside the workplace, the pressure to work longer hours, the need to cope with new work practices, and higher customer expectations, have placed increased stress on many workers. The result of this intensification is an increasing demand from employees for organisations to put in place systems and programmes to assist them in achieving a better work-life balance. **Panel 2.1** presents findings from the *2007 Work-Life Balance in Ireland* study, which highlight the number of hours respondents report spending in the different domains of their life. The study found that, on average, respondents worked more than three hours per week above their contracted hours, demonstrating the trend towards longer working hours.

Panel 2.1: Working & Living: How Employees Spend their Time

The 2007 *Work-Life Balance in Ireland* study explored the amount of time respondents spend in the various domains of life, including work, family / childcare, recreation, and community activities. There were significant differences reported for men and women: men, on average, spend more time in paid employment per week compared with women (42 *versus* 36 hours) and women spend more time engaging in family / household activities compared with men (24 hours v*ersus* 15 hours per week).

Activity / Average house per week:

- Paid work: 38.7.
- Family / housework: 19.9.
- Recreational activities / hobbies: 9.3.
- Community activities: 2.0.

A high percentage of respondents reported that community was important to them; nonetheless, the average time given to community activities is only two hours per week for both men and women. Given the increasing focus at Government level on citizenship, the fact that 48% of respondents report spending no time at all engaged in community activities is a worrying trend.

Source: 2007 Work-Life Balance in Ireland *study.*

---

[13] O'Connell *et al.* (2003).
[14] CIPD (2003).

Employee Expectations

Another interesting development in relation to employee expectations has been the entrance of Generation Y into the workforce. Generation Y are those individuals born after 1978 and these young, educated workers have very different expectations regarding the nature and type of work they are willing to undertake. This generation has been described as 'working to live rather than living to work', unlike their predecessors. The result is a generation of workers who are keen to have flexible working terms, understand that there is no guarantee of a job for life and, therefore, the best that an organisation can offer is challenging work, with the option to develop further transferable skills.

Outside the workplace, it is fair to state that many people are finding it difficult to provide care for children and other dependents, to commute to work because of rising traffic congestion and inadequate investment in the public transport infrastructure, and to find enough time for their personal lives. There is a growing reluctance on the part of employees simply to accept these as a given, and so we have witnessed an increased questioning by employees of why they work, where they work and what they expect from their working lives.

In sum, a broad array of external societal factors, internal organisational factors, and individual employee factors has acted to focus attention on employee work-life balance as an important human resource management policy in the workplace. As employees place greater demands on employers and organisations in the quest to better balance their work and non-working life, it is useful to review how such work-life balance policies and practices impact on the business.

The Business Case

The findings of the *2007 Work–Life Balance in Ireland* study asked the participating line managers for their perceptions of the benefits of operating work-life balance practices in their organisations. **Table 2.4** below outlines their responses ranked by order of importance and by sector.

Table 2.4: Benefits of Operating Work-Life Balance Practices, as Reported by Line Managers in the Private & Public Sectors

Private Sector	Public Sector
1. Improves well-being of employees 2. Increases retention of employees 3. Creates a positive culture in the organisation 4. Increases productivity 5. An advantage in attracting and retaining staff 6. Increases motivation and commitment	1. Improves well-being of employees 2. Increases retention of employees 3. Reduces levels of absenteeism 4. Increases productivity 5. Increases motivation and satisfaction 6. An advantage when attracting and retaining staff 7. Greater staff co-operation and flexibility

Source: 2007 Work-Life Balance in Ireland *study.*

Employee Well-being

In both the public and private sectors, middle / line managers perceived the number one benefit of operating work-life balance practices as being the improvement of the overall well-being of employees. The qualitative feedback from managers reported that the staff who availed of such programmes or initiatives appeared happier in their work, more contented and less stressed in their role. This was believed by many of the managers to lead to an increased positive morale amongst these workers.

Employee Retention

The second benefit reported by managers in both the public and private sectors was the ability of work-life balance initiatives to improve retention of key employees. This is in line with commonly-reported benefits of work-life balance initiatives and has been supported by a number of other research studies. The ability to attract and retain key or star employees is crucial in a tight labour market and, increasingly, organisations are realising that financial incentives alone are not sufficient. The change in employee expectations has led to the need for organisations to be more creative in terms of their offering to employees. The battle to be seen as an 'employer of choice' has intensified and star employees are looking at the whole package in terms of what an employer has to offer. This still includes traditional elements of the reward package but it is also about the non-financial elements. Star employees are acutely aware of the fact that no job is for life anymore. They have embraced the idea of the psychological contract and are very clear in terms of what they expect in return for investing their skills and knowledge in an organisation.

Key questions for the knowledge worker when making career decisions tend to focus on the following:

- What development opportunities does this organisation have to offer?
- What type of experience will I gain while working with this organisation?
- What transferable skills will I develop while here?
- How flexible is this organisation in its approach to meeting my needs? How flexible is it in terms of allowing me to work from home? to take extended leave? and will it support my further formal education?

Employee Morale & Absenteeism

There is a difference in the perceptions of managers in the public and private sectors in relation to the third most important benefit of operating work-life balance arrangements. Private sector managers reported that WLB initiatives assisted in creating a positive culture within the organisation. This is in contrast with the public sector managers who reported that WLB initiatives lead to reduced levels of absenteeism. What we can conclude is that the introduction of work-life balance initiatives and programmes is viewed as assisting organisations in creating the right kind of culture and environment, which allows employees to work in a manner that has mutual benefits for them and their organisations.

Absenteeism is without question a major issue for organisations. A report on absenteeism by the Small Firms Association in 2005 found that Irish firms lose the equivalent of 5 million working days per year as a result of staff sick days, at a cost of €550 million.[15] Contrary to popular belief, consulting group Mercer found that 60% of absenteeism is for legitimate health reasons. The cost savings of a 1% drop in absence rates

---

[15]   Small Firms Association (2005).

for a medium-sized company can amount to €250,000 on sick pay and overtime. The World Health Organisation predicts that, by 2020, five of the top 10 medical problems worldwide will be stress-related.[16] In this context, work-life balance initiatives can play a significant role in creating a positive culture within organisations whereby absenteeism can be reduced.

Increased Productivity

Both the public and private sector managers surveyed in the *2007 Work-Life Balance in Ireland* study noted increased productivity as the fourth potential benefit. This is a somewhat controversial point, as the evidence supporting such a claim remains mainly anecdotal in nature. The absence of hard financial evidence has re-inforced resistance by some business leaders to the idea of the potential benefits of WLB initiatives. This problem is further exacerbated by the inability of researchers to isolate and control for other factors or outside effects that could impact on WLB initiatives and means that this debate is likely to continue.

Attracting Employees

Middle / line managers in both public and private sector organisations viewed WLB initiatives as providing them with a competitive advantage over their rivals when it comes to attracting key staff members. Increasingly, organisations are finding that the people they employ are the true differentiating factor. In an ever-increasingly competitive business environment, organisations are constantly seeking new ways of achieving such competitive advantage.[17] According to the 'resource-based view of the firm',[18] organisations' offerings need to be judged by their customers as either sufficiently rare, valuable, inimitable, and / or non-substitutable. While it is relatively easy to copy or imitate a competitor's product, or indeed their business model, it is not possible to replicate their human capital to the same extent. Thus, the attraction and retention of key employees is increasing in its importance as a source of competitive advantage.

Staff Motivation & Commitment

The final benefits of operating WLB programmes, reported by both public and private sector managers, tend to focus on the areas of increased motivation and commitment and greater staff co-operation and flexibility. These perceived benefits are often cited in the literature on WLB as being potential benefits and, certainly, there is anecdotal evidence to support this assertion. The notion of the psychological contract between employer and employee is relevant here. Employees who believe that their employer is interested in understanding their needs, and is committed to assisting and supporting them, are more likely to respond in a positive way. This, in turn, is likely to translate into increased levels of employee motivation, commitment, and greater staff co-operation.

---

[16] Belshaw (2004).
[17] Litz & Stewart (2000).
[18] Barney (1991).

Organisational Reluctance to Introduce Work-Life Balance Initiatives

While it is tempting to focus only on the potential positives and reported benefits of actively engaging in work-life balance initiatives, the reality is that there can be organisational reluctance to the introduction of some of these initiatives. Some of the most common factors that hinder WLB initiatives are presented in **Figure 2.2**.

Figure 2.2: Factors Associated with Organisational Resistance to Work-Life Balance Initiatives

Cost: The Bottom Line

The primary reason advanced for reluctance on the part of organisations to embrace WLB initiatives fully is concern for the bottom line. Despite anecdotal evidence and numerous studies demonstrating the potentially powerful mutual benefits for both employers and employees, organisations are reluctant to adopt such policies out of fear of the consequence they may have both in the short and longer term. It is unfair to dismiss this concern out of hand, particularly in the case of small and medium-sized firms. The fear is genuine and the economic impact of offering such initiatives is not without financial costs. The business case advanced for the introduction of WLB initiatives, however, argues that, while there are costs, direct or indirect, associated with the implementation of the majority of work-life balance initiatives, the advantages and associated cost savings to the business far outweigh the costs.

Use & Uptake

Organisations are often fearful that, once they implement WLB initiatives, they will have little control over who can, and will, avail of these initiatives. Organisations need to be clear about what initiatives they are prepared to offer, and to whom. A clear and well-designed policy to support any work-life balance initiative is recommended. This policy should be clearly communicated to employees and a fair and transparent decision-making mechanism should be outlined within this policy (see **Chapters 3** and **4** for more details).

The reasons why an employee is granted or refused permission to participate in a WLB programme should be documented and relayed to that employee. Ideally, employees should have the right to appeal any decision regarding access to such programmes or initiatives if they are unhappy.

Impact on Staff Not Availing of Work-Life Balance Programmes

Often, organisations are concerned about the impact that WLB initiatives will have on the remaining workforce. In particular, managers and supervisors are cited as having concerns regarding the increased workload that results from managing such initiatives.

Related to this point is potential 'employee backlash'. This phenomenon has recently come to the fore, particularly in the US, where commentators have reported increased employee dissatisfaction with those colleagues who avail of WLB programmes. Employee backlash tends to arise where WLB programmes or initiatives are limited to specific sub-groups of employees, for example, women with children. **Panel 2.2** refers to some findings from the *2007 Work-Life Balance in Ireland* study, which highlight the challenge of ensuring WLB eligibility criteria are seen to be fair.

Panel 2.2: Perceived Fairness of Work-Life Balance Programme Eligibility Criteria

Findings from the *2007 Work-Life Balance in Ireland* study report that a significant percentage of middle / line managers, particularly in the public sector where more temporal arrangements (i.e. reduced hours) are offered, tend to report that WLB initiatives are unfair to some employees. This view was demonstrated by the following interview quotations:

"There is an issue about equity and fairness – employees who do not have children can feel discriminated against when they cannot avail of certain initiatives e.g. term time." - Middle / line manager, public sector

"There is some element of "carrying the can" for full-time employees." - Middle / line manager, public sector

"Employees who are left behind [employees not availing of WLB initiatives] have an increased workload and there is an expectation for them to take on the extra work." - Middle / line manager, public sector

Source: 2007 Work-Life Balance in Ireland *study.*

Incompatibility with Business Model / Working Hours

A final organisational barrier cited is the incompatibility of the WLB initiatives with the business model that the organisation has chosen to adopt. It is critical that the business model of the organisation is considered; however, it is highly unlikely that an organisation finds itself in the position whereby it cannot enact any WLB policies (see **Chapter 4** for details on the various WLB policies and practices that exist). The reality is that, while it may not be possible to offer working from home, for example, in a face-to-face service environment, there are other WLB policies that could be implemented.

As a general rule, organisations that approach WLB in an open manner, and that are prepared to look at what their employees want alongside what their business model requires, are more likely to reap the many positive mutual benefits that WLB programmes can deliver.

Why Employees Avail of Work-Life Balance Initiatives

The *2007 Work-Life Balance in Ireland* study also sought to ascertain the reasons why employees across both the public and private sectors engaged, or did not engage, in work-life balance initiatives. The findings are presented in **Table 2.5** and list in rank order the most often-cited reasons employees report for using WLB initiatives.

Table 2.5: Employees' Reasons for Engaging in Work-Life Balance Initiatives, by Sector

Private Sector	Public Sector
1. Commuting / traffic.	1. Childcare.
2. Childcare.	2. Need / want more personal time.
3. Need / want more personal time.	3. Commuting / traffic.
4. Eldercare.	4. Eldercare.

Source: 2007 Work-Life Balance in Ireland *study.*

Both public and private sector employees generally reported the same reasons as to why they engage in WLB initiatives. These reasons, while ordered slightly differently, tended to reflect the same concerns.

Commuting / Traffic

Employees in the private sector stated that commuting and traffic issues were their number one reason for availing of WLB initiatives. Private sector employees evidently find a flexible approach to their working day extremely beneficial in terms of improving their work-life balance. Typically, these initiatives tend to include, but are not limited to:

- Late / early start and finishing times, so as to avoid congestion problems.
- Ability to work from home for all, or part, of the week.
- Ability to log on from home for the rush hours of each day and then proceed to the office when the traffic congestion has calmed.

A recent report, published by O2, on senior executives in small and medium-sized businesses, found that some 30% of these executives reported working at least a day a month from home. An improved work-life balance was cited by respondents as one of the main benefits to them of this type of atypical working.

Commuting / traffic was further down the list of cited reasons why public sector employees engage in WLB initiatives – ranked third. This is likely to reflect the fact that the public sector, for the most part, does operate a system of flexible working arrangements in relation to start and finishing times and has done so for some time. Pilot studies have also been initiated in terms of extending atypical forms of working, such as e-working and working from home; however, this is limited to certain departments and roles within these organisations.

giv   nat organisations would be prudent to
av   res, which would allow employees to
in   loyee who sits in traffic for two hours
be   be highly motivated by the time they
th   der alternative working arrangements
                                                                        s or location.

C

C   yees engaged in WLB initiatives in both
tł   ! respectively). The issue of childcare
                                                                        our national agenda for some time. The
temptation to frame this issue as a solely female problem is very real, but misguided. We
have witnessed the increased desire of fathers to play an active role in the lives of their
children, and Irish society has changed in this regard over the past two decades. Fathers are
much more hands-on today in their parenting role than they were 20 years ago and there is
a real desire on the part of this new generation of fathers to be there for key events in their
children's lives. Indeed, it has been reported that 82% of Irish fathers would like to spend
more time with their families and so it is likely that we will see an increase in number of
requests from male employees seeking to access parental leave.[19]

The 2007 *Work-Life Balance in Ireland* study found that some middle / line managers, in
particular in the private sector, who were fathers, were dissatisfied with their own WLB
because of the additional hours they were expected to work and cited their dissatisfaction
with not being able to spend more time with their families.

Changing Employee Priorities & Expectations

In the previous section, we discussed the individual factors that are creating a momentum
for the introduction of WLB initiatives in organisations. One of the factors cited is changing
employee expectations; this point is reinforced by the finding that both public and private
sector employees cited the need for more personal time as a reason for engaging in WLB
initiatives (ranked number 3 for private sector employees and number 2 for public sector
employees). The desire of employees to have a better quality of life is clearly evident. We
must be careful not to assume that this finding only relates to those employees with a
family, but rather it speaks to all employees who are happy to work hard but are not
content to let work dominate their lives. It appears that we are moving from a mentality of
'living to work' to 'working to live'. Work is now viewed as a means to an end, rather than
an end in, and of, itself.

Eldercare

Finally, employees reported eldercare as another reason for availing of work-life balance
initiatives. Eldercare is an increasingly important factor impacting upon employees' lives
and is likely to continue to do so as we witness the aging of the population and the limited
number of resources available to deal with the phenomenon. While employees have some
rights under the Carer's Leave Act 2001, it is likely that organisations will see increasing
requests from employees in need of assistance to deal with this issue. **Case study 2.1**, from
the Department of Justice, Equality & Law Reform, presents some interesting views on the
needs of employees to avail of carer's leave.

---

[19]   Fine-David & Clarke (2002).

CASE STUDY 2.1

Department of Justice, Equality & Law Reform
Work-Life Balance & Caring for Elderly Relatives

Martina Colville, a senior HR Manager working in the Department of Justice, Equality & Law Reform discusses the growing needs of employees to avail of carer's leave to care for elderly relatives.

"For most people, when asked what they associate with the term 'work-life balance', they invariably speak of issues regarding mothers and children. However, the reality for many of us, in a society where people live longer, is that work-life balance in future just as easily might conjure up the words 'elderly' and 'carer'. It is increasingly our experience in the Department of Justice, Equality & Law Reform that people are seeking work arrangements to facilitate being able to care for an elderly parent (or both parents) at home. In cases such as this, flexibility around work patterns is important, particularly where residential care is not an option.

"While carer's leave is available for some staff, the reality is that it is not economically viable for many. In addition, staff may find themselves reluctantly in the position of carer for an elderly relative and therefore, in so far as is possible, they will try to maintain as strong a linkage as possible to their job. Flexibility around the work arrangements facilitates them in this regard.

"As an organisation, we could take the view that there is no added value for us in facilitating people who may need to care for an elderly relative. The reality, however, is that the age profile for a staff member who finds themselves in the caring situation is likely to mean that they are an experienced and knowledgeable member of staff. The cost of facilitating the flexible working arrangement potentially is significantly less than the investment in recruitment and training of a new member of staff.

"Currently, we are not able to provide statistical evidence to support our experience. We are revising our applications procedure to enable us to capture information that, in the future, will identify the reasons why staff may be availing of particular work life balance options."

– taken from an interview with Martina Colville, Senior HR Manager, Department of Justice, Equality & Law Reform.

Why Employees Do Not Avail of Work-Life Balance Initiatives

Again, drawing from the *2007 Work-Life Balance in Ireland* study, **Table 2.6** summarises the responses of both public and private sector employees as to why they do **not** engage in work-life balance initiatives, where available. These findings highlight some interesting perceptions among employees as to the negative consequence of availing of such policies. If we are truly committed to improving the work-life balance of employees, then we need to seriously tackle each of these issues.

Table 2.6: Employees' Reasons for Not Engaging in Work-Life Balance Initiatives, by Sector

Private Sector	Public Sector
1. Not available to me.	1. Financial considerations.
2. Job does not lend itself to flexible practices.	2. Already satisfied with work-life balance.
3. Financial considerations.	3. Negative career consequences.
4. Negative career consequences.	4. Not available to me.
5. Already satisfied with work-life balance.	5. Job does not lend itself to flexible practices.

Source: 2007 Work-Life Balance in Ireland *study.*

Financial Considerations

There appears to be a general perception among both public and private sector employees that availing of work-life balance programmes or initiatives is likely to have a negative impact, in terms of their financial well-being. Clearly, an employee opting to avail of reduced working hours naturally will experience a drop in salary to reflect this fact. However, the possibilities in terms of availing of atypical forms of work, which do not necessarily have a negative financial impact, appear to be overlooked by the majority of workers (these atypical forms of work are discussed in greater detail in **Chapter 4**).

Career Consequences

The concern that most commentators have is that availing of WLB initiatives is interpreted by employees and employers alike as an indication that the employee is no longer fully committed to their work-role, or the organisation, and has little or no desire to advance their career. It is very worrying that negative career consequences was cited as the number four and number three reasons by employees in the private and public sector respectively, as to why they do not engage in WLB initiatives. This perception of WLB as a career-ending step needs to be addressed, if we are to make any real progress in terms of improving employee WLB.

Lack of Availability

A commonly-cited barrier to the introduction of WLB initiatives is the argument that the business model does not support such flexibility. While this is a legitimate limitation in certain cases (for example, manufacturing and face-to-face service roles), it is sometimes the case that organisations do not seriously question the extent to which the operating model can be made more flexible. It is hard to imagine that, given the breadth and depth of possible work-life balance initiatives available, none would be suitable. Yet, the *2007 Work-Life Balance in Ireland* study found that the lack of availability of work-life balance initiatives was cited as a main reason for not engaging in WLB initiatives among public and private sector employees.

On the positive side, some employees reported not availing of work-life balance initiatives as they were already satisfied with the balance in their lives. Interestingly, public sector workers ranked this as the number two reason for not availing of such initiatives while it was further down the private sector employee reasons at number five.

Political & Social Developments in the Work-Life Balance Agenda

While the previous sections of this chapter refer to individual and organisational factors influencing the work-life balance agenda, the Government is also a key player. Social and public policy, as well as legislative developments, significantly influence work-life balance policy and practice.

Under *Towards 2016*,[20] the latest national social partnership agreement, the Government re-affirmed its commitment to the work of the National Framework Committee for Work-Life Balance, initially established under the earlier national social partnership agreement, *Programme for Prosperity & Fairness* (PPF).[21] Under PPF, the Government stated that it was committed to identifying options with the potential to meet the many diverse needs of employers and their employees, whilst recognising that this area can be especially problematic. In order to be effective, the Government felt such options must meet the following objectives: "enhance the opportunity to reconcile work and family life; and contribute to the effective and efficient operation of the enterprise".[22] In the light of this, the role of the National Framework Committee for Work-Life Balance is to continue under *Towards 2016* to support and facilitate the development of family-friendly policies aimed at assisting in the reconciliation of work and family life at the level of the enterprise.

The Government's commitment to improving the work-life balance of its citizens is clearly outlined in its vision for 'People of Working Age'. In this section of *Towards 2016*, the Government states that: "the parties to this agreement share a vision of an Ireland where all people of working age have sufficient income and opportunity to participate as fully as possible in economic and social life and where all individuals and their families are supported by a range of quality public services to enhance their quality of life and well-being".[23]

The parties to the agreement go even further, when they state that it is the objective of the Government that "every person of working age would have access to lifelong learning, a sense of personal security in a changing work environment and an opportunity to balance work and family commitments consistent with business needs".[24]

In addition, there are a number of key pieces of legislation that provide a floor of statutory rights relating to family-friendly / work-life balance issues; these are outlined below.

---

[20] Department of An Taoiseach (2006).
[21] Department of An Taoiseach (2000).
[22] Department of An Taoiseach (2000), page 42.
[23] Department of An Taoiseach (2006), page 47.
[24] Department of An Taoiseach (2006), page 47.

What Does the Law Require Employers to Do?

In relation to work-life balance or family-friendly working arrangements, a number of different legislative instruments are relevant. It is essential, however, that organisations recognise fully the difference between the statutory obligations they have to their employees and any additional non-statutory elements they may opt to introduce.

To assist managers in identifying their legal obligations, the following section briefly outlines a number of current pieces of legislation that apply in the broad area of work-life balance. This is not a legal text and so the discussion in relation to legislation is limited to how these instruments potentially impact on organisations and their adoption of work-life balance initiatives.

Table 2.7: Summary of Statutory Instruments Promoting Better Work-Life Balance

- Protection of Employees (Part-Time Work) Act 2001.
- Organisation of Working Time Act 1997.
- Maternity Protection Act 1994 and Maternity Protection (Amendment) Act 2004.
- Parental Leave Act 1998 and Parental Leave (Amendment) Act 2006 (including *force majeure*).
- Adoptive Parents Leave Act 1995 and Adoptive Leave Act 2005.
- Carer's Leave Act 2001.

Protection of Employees (Part-Time Work)

The rights of part-time employees in Ireland are protected in law through the Protection of Employees (Part-Time Work) Act 2001. The purpose of the Act is to ensure that part-time employees are not treated in a less favourable manner than a comparable full-time employee, unless there are objective reasons for such treatment. Where an employer tries to justify less favourable treatment on objective grounds, he / she has to show that the difference in treatment is based on grounds other than the part-time status of the employee, is a legitimate purpose of the employer, and is appropriate and necessary for that purpose. What may be considered as not being objective grounds in relation to regular part-time workers, however, may be considered objective grounds in relation to casual part-time workers.

A part-time employee in Ireland is defined in the Act as "an employee whose normal hours of work are less than the normal hours of work of an employee who is a comparable employee in relation to him or her". A comparable employee means a full-time employee (of the same or opposite sex) to whom a part-time employee compares himself / herself. A part-time worker no longer has to have 13 continuous weeks' service and no longer has to work a minimum of 8 hours per week in order to qualify for protection under the Act.

Following the introduction of the *Code of Practice on Access to Part-time Work*[25] in 2006, best practice for employers is to have policies on improving access to part-time work. Although the *Code of Practice* is not a legal obligation on employers, it aims to encourage employers and employees to consider part-time work and provides guidance on procedures to improve access to part-time work for those employees who wish to work on a part-time basis. In general, employers should consider how to introduce opportunities for part-time work and should maximise the range of posts available for part-time work.

---

[25] LRC (2006).

It is important to note, however, that a full-time employee does not have a statutory right to change to part-time employment or other flexible working arrangements, such as job-sharing. The granting of a request for part-time work remains a matter for an employer and employee to agree between them. The request for part-time working arrangements should be given serious consideration on the part of the employer and due consideration should be given to factors such as the personal circumstances of the employee, the implications for the organisation, the number of part-time employees already in the organisation, the equal opportunities policy and staffing needs of the organisation. It is essential that any request is considered in a non-discriminatory manner and in accordance with employment equality legislation.

Flexible hours and flexible working arrangements are generally at the discretion of individual employers and are not governed by specific legislation. People who share a job are viewed as part-time workers and have all the statutory entitlements of part-time workers.

Organisation of Working Time

The Organisation of Working Time Act 1997 outlines an employer's obligations to its employees in relation to rest breaks, maximum working hours, Sunday working and holidays. Again, the approach an employer adopts in relation to breaks and working hours must not have the effect of treating part-time staff less favourably relative to their full-time counterparts.

Maternity Leave

The Maternity Protection Act 1994 and Maternity Protection (Amendment) Act 2004 currently entitle a pregnant employee to 26 consecutive weeks' leave, with the option of taking an additional 16 weeks' unpaid leave. In addition, a pregnant employee who is attending antenatal and postnatal care is entitled to time off from work to attend such appointments, without loss of pay. However, employees must inform their employer in writing of the time and date of the appointments no later than two weeks before the appointment date. An expectant father of a child (if he is employed under a contract of employment) is entitled to time off from work, without loss of pay, to attend the last two ante-natal classes in a set before the birth.

An employee's entitlement to pay during maternity leave depends on the terms of the original employment contract. Employers are not obliged to pay women on maternity leave, nor is there any obligation for an employer to 'top up' a woman's salary – that is, to add to the welfare maternity benefit payment she receives so that she is at no financial loss.

An employee is entitled after maternity leave to return to work with the same employer, to the same job under the same contract and under the terms and conditions that are (i) not less favourable than those that would have applied to her and (ii) incorporate any improvement to the terms and conditions to which she would have been entitled if she had not been absent.

An employee on maternity leave is entitled to leave for any public holidays that occur during the period of maternity leave (including additional maternity leave). Time spent on maternity leave (including additional maternity leave) is treated as though the employee has been in employment, and this time can be used to accumulate annual leave and public holiday entitlement.

If a pregnant employee suffers a stillbirth or miscarriage any time after the 24th week of pregnancy, she is entitled to full maternity leave of a basic period of 26 weeks and 16 weeks of additional maternity leave.

There is a health and safety requirement on an employer to carry out separate risk assessments in relation to pregnant employees and those who have recently given birth or are breastfeeding. If there are particular risks, these should be either removed or the employee moved away from them. If neither of these options is possible, the employee should be given health and safety leave from work. During health and safety leave, employers must pay employees their normal wages for the first three weeks, after which health and safety benefit may be paid. The Health & Safety Authority should be contacted in relation to any questions on pregnant employees at work.

Parental Leave

The Parental Leave Act 1998, as amended by the Parental Leave (Amendment) Act 2006, allows parents in Ireland to take parental leave from employment in respect of children of a certain age. A person acting *in loco parentis* is also eligible.

Since 18 May 2006, leave can be taken in respect of a child up to eight years of age. If a child was adopted between the age of six and eight, leave in respect of that child may be taken up to two years after the date of the adoption order. In the case of a child with a disability, leave may be taken up to 16 years of age. Parental leave is available for each child and amounts to a total of 14 weeks per child. Where an employee has more than one child, parental leave is limited to 14 weeks in a 12-month period. This can be longer, if the employer agrees. (This restriction does not apply in the case of a multiple birth, such as twins or triplets.)

The 14 weeks per child may be taken in one continuous period, or in separate blocks of a minimum of six weeks. If the employer agrees, an employee can separate their leave into periods of days or even hours. Both parents have an equal, separate entitlement to parental leave.

Employees are not entitled to pay from their employer while on parental leave, nor are they entitled to any social welfare payment. Taking parental leave does not affect other employment rights, however. Apart from the loss of wages, the position of the parent remains as if no parental leave had been taken. This means, for example, that time spent on parental leave can be used to accumulate annual leave entitlement.

As a general rule, there is a requirement to have been working for a year before being entitled to parental leave. However, if the child is very near the age threshold and the employee has been working for the employer for more than three months but less than one year, then they are entitled to *pro rata* parental leave, on the basis of one week's leave for every month of employment completed. If an individual changes job and has used part of their parental leave allowance, they can use the remainder after one year's employment with their new employer, provided the child is still under the qualifying age.

Apart from a refusal on the grounds on non-entitlement, an employer may also postpone the leave for up to six months. This must be done before the confirmation document is signed. Grounds for such a postponement include lack of cover or the fact that other employees are already on parental leave. Normally, only one postponement is allowed.

Employees who opt to take parental leave are entitled to return to their job after their leave, unless it is not reasonably practicable for the employer to allow them to return to their old job. If an employer wishes to invoke this clause, they must offer the employee a suitable alternative on terms no less favourable compared with the previous job, including any improvement in pay or other conditions that occurred while the employee was on parental leave.

Force Majeure *Leave*

The law in Ireland gives an employee a limited right to leave from work in time of family crisis, otherwise known as *force majeure*. This right comes under the Parental Leave Act 1998, as amended by the Parental Leave (Amendment) Act 2006, which gives an employee a limited right to leave from work. It arises where, for urgent family reasons, the immediate presence of the employee is indispensable or as a result of an injury to, or illness involving, a close family member.

The Act defines 'a close family member' as a child or adopted child of the employee, the husband / wife / partner of the employee, the parent or grandparent of the employee, brother or sister of the employee. The close family member may also include a person to whom the employee has a duty of care (that is, he / she is acting *in loco parentis*) and a person in a relationship of domestic dependency with the employee, including a same-sex partner (since 18 May 2006).

The maximum amount of leave is three days in any 12-month period or five days in a 36-month period. There is an entitlement to be paid while on *force majeure* leave and protection against dismissal is provided under the Unfair Dismissal Acts.

Adoptive Parents' Leave

Under the Adoptive Leave Act 1995, and amended by the Adoptive Leave Act 2005, only the adoptive mother is entitled to avail of adoptive leave from employment, except in the case where a male is the sole adopter. The new adoptive parents' leave, as from 1 March 2007, is 24 weeks, with the option to take an additional 16 weeks' unpaid leave.

The Adoptive Leave Act 2005, which came into effect on 28 November 2005, introduced some important changes and additional rights for adoptive parents. In line with maternity leave rights, adoptive parents saw all employment rights (except remuneration and superannuation benefits) associated with the employment, such as annual leave and seniority, as protected during additional adoptive leave. Adopting parents are now entitled to paid time off work to attend preparation classes and pre-adoption meetings with social workers or Health Service Executive (HSE) officials required during the pre-adoption process. An employee's absence from work on additional unpaid adoptive leave counts for all employment rights (except remuneration and superannuation benefits) associated with the employment, such as annual leave and seniority. The employee has the same rights to return to work as with maternity leave and must give four weeks' notice of the intention to return. An adoptive parent is entitled to return to the job they had immediately before the leave, unless this is not reasonably practicable for the employer. Where this is the case, the employer must offer a suitable and appropriate alternative. The terms and conditions of the alternative, and the capacity under which the adoptive parent is to be employed, must not be less favourable than their job prior to going on leave. Adoptive parents are protected against unfair dismissal for claiming their rights under adoptive leave legislation.

Carer's Leave

The Carer's Leave Act 2001 allows employees in Ireland to leave their employment temporarily to provide full-time care for someone in need of full-time care and attention. Since 24 March 2006, the minimum period of leave is 13 weeks and the maximum period is 104 weeks (previously 65 weeks). Carer's leave from employment is unpaid but the Act ensures that those who propose to avail of carer's leave will have their jobs kept open for them for the duration of the leave.

In order to be eligible to apply for carer's leave, the employee must have worked for the employer for a continuous period of 12 months. The person in need of care must be deemed to be in need of full-time care and attention by a deciding officer of the Department of Social & Family Affairs. The decision by the Department is reached on the basis of information provided by the family doctor (GP) of the person who is in need of care. The criteria used are such as to render the person so disabled as to require continuous supervision and frequent assistance throughout the day in connection with their normal personal needs for example, help to eat, drink, wash or dress, or continuous supervision in order to avoid danger to themselves. An interesting aspect of the Carer's Leave Act is that the person that requires the care need not be a family member or spouse but could be a friend or colleague.

Carer's leave must be taken in one continuous period of 104 weeks or for a number of periods not exceeding a total of 104 weeks. If the carer does not opt to take the leave in one continuous period, there must be a gap of at least six weeks between the periods of carer's leave. An employer may refuse (on reasonable grounds) to allow an employee to take a period of carer's leave less than 13 weeks in duration. Where an employer refuses this leave, he or she must specify in writing the grounds for refusing such leave.

An employee cannot move from one period of carer's leave to another upon the termination of one period of leave. That is to say, an employee cannot commence another period of carer's leave to care for a different person until a period of 6 months has elapsed since the termination of the previous period of carer's leave.

This section has set out the statutory provisions and entitlements relating to personal and family life. While this legislative context provides the statutory framework within which organisations must operate, this guide focuses on the work-life balance and flexible working arrangements organisations use at their discretion and describes a model of best practice to guide managers and organisations on the design, implementation, and evaluation of these discretionary polices and practices.

Chapter Summary

The rise of work-life balance can be traced back to a number of external societal, internal organisational and individual factors which have combined to create a growing pressure for the introduction of work-life balance policies and initiatives. This chapter identified and discussed each of these factors, in order to provide a contextual background against which to discuss and examine work-life balance.

Drawing on the most recent work-life balance data in Ireland, the chapter referred to some of the findings of the 2007 Work-Life Balance in Ireland *study to establish the case for work-life balance. The argument that WLB is just another 'faddish management technique' is dispelled. Rather than a passing trend, the discussion of each of the factors contributing to the pressure for WLB reinforces the likelihood that WLB will continue to remain a pivotal issue for society, organisations and individual employees alike into the future.*

The next chapter will begin to explore the factors that lead to effective work-life balance policy and programme design in organisations.

3: Designing WLB Policies & Programmes

"The challenge is for the organisation to meet its commitments. However, when employees are focused and take individual accountability and responsibility, flexible working practices can be achieved."
– Middle / line manager, **2007 Work-Life Balance in Ireland** *study*

This chapter examines the various issues to be considered when designing WLB policies and programmes.

Effective design is critical to subsequent implementation of work-life balance policies and practices. It is important for organisations to identify clearly a work-life balance strategy that then determines the framework within which the work-life balance policies and practices operate. Once the work-life balance strategy has been determined, the context and business needs must be explored to establish what work-life balance policies and practices suit the organisation in terms of its culture and business needs. It is important also that employee needs are considered, to ensure a match between what the organisation proposes to offer and what employees require in terms of managing work and personal life demands better. The chapter presents a framework for establishing employee work-life balance needs.

The final section of the chapter identifies the stakeholders who should be consulted in designing work-life balance policies and practices. Thus, this chapter deals with stages 1 to 4 of the best practice work-life balance design, implementation, and evaluation model that was presented in **Figure 1.1**.

Work-Life Balance Design: Towards A Holistic Approach

A broad range of work-life balance practices, programmes and policies are available to organisations. It is essential that work-life balance initiatives are developed in a holistic manner whereby there is a clear strategy across the organisation underpinning work-life balance design, implementation, and evaluation. The needs of the business, management and employees must be taken into consideration when developing work-life balance programmes. It is critical to adopt a multi-stakeholder approach to design and implementation, whereby all relevant stakeholders in work-life balance (senior management, middle / line managers, employees, and employee representative groups) are consulted. The culture of the organisation is also an important factor to consider when designing WLB initiatives.

Figure 3.1 presents a model of the four stages that organisations should follow when designing work-life balance policies and practices. It offers a holistic approach to designing work-life balance policies and programmes, incorporating multi-perspectives at all levels in the firm. A variety of options are available to firms in terms of the various work-life balance practices and arrangements they can make available and organisations must choose the most appropriate given their own strategy, business, and employee / management needs. Organisations need to address each of the four design stages in **Figure 3.1** before effective decisions regarding policy choice and implementation can be made. Each of these design issues is discussed in turn below.

Figure 3.1: Designing Work-Life Balance Policies & Programmes

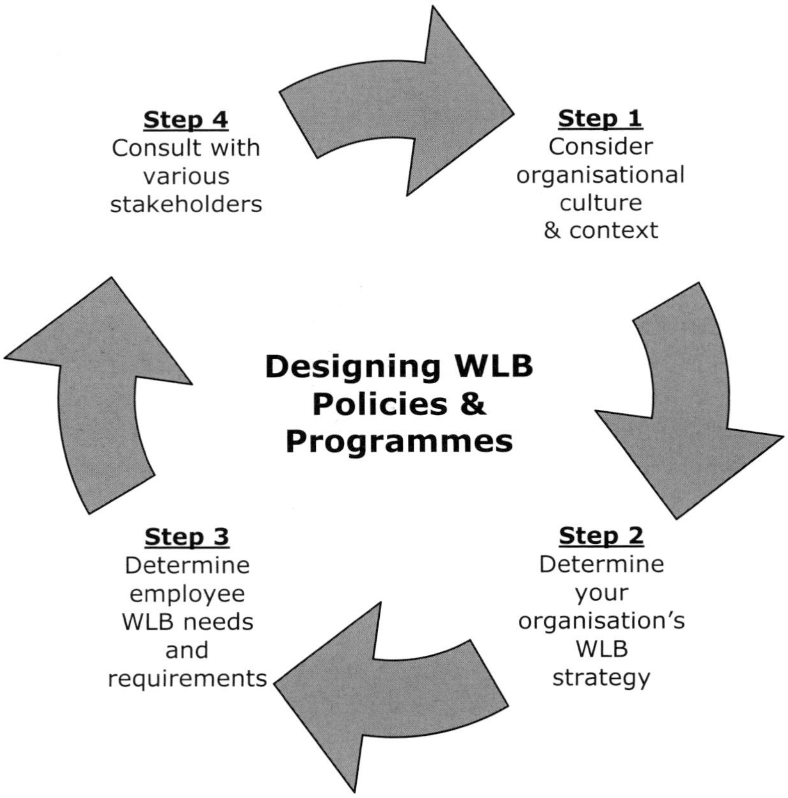

Step 4
Consult with various stakeholders

Step 1
Consider organisational culture & context

Designing WLB Policies & Programmes

Step 3
Determine employee WLB needs and requirements

Step 2
Determine your organisation's WLB strategy

Step 1: Consider the Business Context & Organisational Culture

The overall strategy for work-life balance will only be determined effectively by taking due cognisance of the business context and realities of the needs of the business. This step is fundamental, since work-life balance policies and programmes will be feasible only if they are aligned to the business needs and business cycle. Thus, some work-life balance policies and programmes will be suitable and others will not. The organisational culture is also an important factor to consider during step 1.

The Business Context

As mentioned above, the reality of the business context, client demands, and the operating cycle of the business will influence significantly the practicality of introducing and managing various work-life balance policies and practices. For example, a flexi-time system is unlikely to be a suitable work-life balance programme available to all employees within a 24 / 7 manufacturing facility, since there will be set shift patterns and hours. Therefore, it is vital that the reality of the business context be taken into consideration as to the feasibility of various work-life balance policies and practices for different employee groups.

The following are some of the issues identified by CIPD[26] as important business context factors that should be explored by organisations wishing to develop successful work-life policies and programmes:

- Identify the business needs, so as to demonstrate to business colleagues how having a work-life strategy will benefit both the business and the workforce.

- Adapt policies to match operational needs, by looking at both employee and business priorities and considering the impact of WLB policies and practices on customers, back-up arrangements to cover absence, and training needs.

- Identify measures for performance, which should be based on outcomes and results at business unit and organisation levels.

Similarly, the Queensland Government Department of Employment & Industrial Relations in Australia[27] suggests that organisations should consider the following operating requirements when exploring the business needs:

- Client contact hours.
- Equipment operating needs.
- Minimum staffing requirements.
- Workflow and workload peaks and troughs.

The choice of work-life balance initiatives must complement these business realities and ensure that the business operating requirements are not affected adversely by the choice of initiatives made available to staff and management. It is important that management undertake feasibility analysis studies of various policies and programmes to ensure the most appropriate are chosen for implementation, given the realities and constraints of the business / organisation.

---

[26] CIPD (2007a).
[27] QGDoEIR (2007).

Organisational Culture & Attitudes

Related to the business needs is the concept of organisational culture and attitudes. While the culture and attitudes relating to work-life balance may be somewhat more intangible and difficult to identify in comparison to the business context issues highlighted above, culture and attitudinal issues nonetheless are important factors affecting work-life balance strategy, policy and practice and should also be considered at step 1.

Organisational culture is an important dimension of organisational life, influencing how people behave in the workplace. Organisational culture refers to the set of beliefs and attitudes regarding the norms and expectations held by members of the organisation that give rise to an understanding of 'how things are done around here'. Organisational culture plays a central role in the design, adoption, and effectiveness of work-life balance policies and programmes. A question that arises in designing and implementing work-life balance arrangements is whether such policies and programmes will work and be effective in a particular organisational culture. Therefore, management should assess the culture and attitudes that prevail within the organisation that have the potential to affect work-life balance policy and practice positively or adversely.

Using the diagnostic framework developed by the Work-Life Balance Network (2004), **Table 3.1** presents an outline of the culture characteristics and attitudes representative of different levels of work-life balance strategy maturity and embeddedness within an organisation. At each level of work-life balance strategy maturity, varying work-life balance cultures and attitudes exist:

- At the **formative** stage, where work-life balance strategy is largely reactive and not seen to be an important HR issue, the focus is on rules and regulations regarding time and attendance, where long working hours and lack of flexibility are accepted habits and practices. Managers act in ways that can affect the work-life balance of employees unfavourably. The culture is one where staff must work long and hard to be seen to be committed.

- At the **broadening** stage, there are still many poor practices that impact negatively on work-life balance, such as a culture of long working hours, early morning and late evening meetings, as identified in the *2007 Work-Life Balance in Ireland* study. However, there are some attitudes and cultural dimensions that have a positive impact on work-life balance (for example, some managers acting as effective work-life balance role models) and assist in WLB strategy and policy becoming more integrated into the business.

- At the **deepening** stage, the culture and attitudes are more conducive to work-life balance. There is greater flexibility to meet individual needs and requirements and some work-life balance practices are available to management and staff. Senior and middle / line management understand the role they play in helping employees to achieve work-life balance.

- At the **mature** stage, organisations have work-life balance policies and programmes well-embedded into the operation of the business. There is a healthy work-life balance culture in existence and the attitudes of staff and management towards those engaging in work-life balance programmes and initiatives is positive. Unnecessarily long working hours are questioned and the concept of 'presenteeism' is challenged. The organisation is responsive to individual employee and business unit needs and the challenges of managing work and personal life are facilitated.

Table 3.1: Work-Life Balance Culture in Operation at Different Stages of Work-Life Balance Evolution

Stage	WLB Culture & Attitudes
Formative	The perception that committed people work long hours. Meetings are routinely arranged outside core hours and continue after hours. Terms and conditions of employment are rigid (for example, express focus on certain time & attendance patterns). Managers enforce rules and discipline and do not understand the need to act as role models for WLB.
Broadening	Terms and conditions of employment are rigid but becoming stratified (for example, part-time staff, jobsharers at lower categories). Managers working within strict policies and procedures, including performance measures. Some managers acting as WLB role models. Meetings are planned to finish within core hours. Flexibility is the exception, rather than the norm. Some senior managers understand the need to act as role models.
Deepening	Performance measurements focus on output, and not necessarily inputs (hours). Terms and conditions are less rigid and more oriented to meet the diverse needs of work units and staff. Some WLB choices available to managers and staff. All managers understand the need to act as role models. Some (50%+) senior managers acting as role models. Flexibility in terms of moving within the organisation to achieve WLB needs. People accessing WLB programmes have equal promotion opportunities.
Mature	Performance measures focus on outputs, including key HR and business indicators. Senior managers act as role models, set an example, and do not routinely work long hours. Questions are asked if people regularly work long hours. Flexible working practices do not negatively impact on career progress. Organisation is flexible and proactive in response to changing business and employee needs.

Source: Adapted from Work-Life Balance Network (2004: 53).

Three key stakeholders influence work-life balance culture in particular:

- **Senior management**: The extent to which senior management buy into work-life balance initiatives and programmes will be an important determinant of the practice of work-life balance across the organisation. If work-life balance is seen to be an important HR issue, then there must be support from senior management to enable the WLB strategy to be translated into practice at the employee level.

  Where senior management embrace WLB in their own approach to work, this will transcend the organisation and be a positive influence affecting the overall WLB culture in the company. If, on the other hand, senior management are seen not to buy into the concept of work-life balance, or to behave in ways that are contradictory to the achievement of work-life balance in practice, this will adversely affect middle / line manager and employee attitude towards work-life balance. Such a culture will result in the WLB strategy and policy being seen to exist only in rhetoric rather than in reality, existing on paper but not functioning effectively in practice.

Where senior management are champions of work-life balance in terms of their attitudes and behaviours, the uptake and usage of various work-life balance practices tends to be higher among employees.

- **Middle / line management**: Research shows that managerial support for work-life balance is a critical factor in work-life balance policy usage and effectiveness.[28] [29] The line manager / supervisor is often the first point of contact for an employee with a query about various HR policies and options, including work-life balance. Middle / line managers, therefore, are a critical lynchpin in translating work-life balance strategy and policy into practice in the following ways:

  - Middle / line manager attitudes towards work-life balance will influence either positively or negatively employee knowledge of work-life balance policies and programmes, as well as eligibility to use these options.

  - Middle / line manager knowledge and awareness of various WLB policies and options will influence their ability to advise employees on various options and policies available to them.

  - Middle / line manager involvement in designing and implementing WLB policies and practices will influence employees' direct experiences of these practices.

Where middle / line managers are supportive of WLB initiatives and encourage employees to avail of the various practices available, there are higher levels of employee uptake of these initiatives and higher levels of satisfaction with work-life balance in general. However, where middle / line managers are not supportive of work-life balance, it is difficult for employees to avail of these programmes, irrespective of the policies that exist. Middle / line managers, therefore, play a critical role in ensuring that work-life balance strategy and policy is enacted into practice.

It is important that middle / line managers are actively involved in the design stage of the work-life balance policies and programmes to ensure their buy-in, support, and understanding of WLB initiatives. A study of two organisations that had introduced work-life balance initiatives found that the lack of support from line managers was a bone of contention for those who were dissatisfied with newly-introduced work-life balance practices.[30]

Thus, middle / line managers influence the work-life balance culture in the organisation as a result of their attitudes, knowledge, experience, and support for work-life balance. Organisations must ensure that middle / line managers are adequately involved in designing as well as implementing work-life balance policies and practices since they are a critical stakeholder in the process (see step 4 in this chapter for more detail).

- **Colleagues / employees**: The third feature of organisational culture affecting work-life balance practice is colleague support for engaging in, and using, work-life balance practices. If peers are supportive of work-life balance, then employees tend to find it easier to use and avail of various WLB initiatives, compared with cultures where there is some resistance from peers or colleagues. Such resistance can arise from a perception that those not availing of WLB initiatives have to work harder or longer as a result of their colleagues using WLB or flexible practices (for example, job-sharing part-time, term-time). 'Employee backlash' can result from perceived inequity in how the WLB

---

[28] McConville & Holden (1999).
[29] Purcell & Hutchinson (2007).
[30] Nord *et al.* (2002).

strategy is implemented. This can cause some resentment among employees and, ultimately, can act as a barrier to the use of various policies.

The degree to which various work-life balance programmes and policies are available to all employee groups is another important factor affecting work-life balance culture within an organisation. In many cases, organisations will not be able to make certain work-life balance programmes available to all staff at all levels. Organisations must consider eligibility issues carefully and clearly communicate to staff the reasons why certain cohorts of employees may be ineligible to use and take up various work-life balance programmes (see **Chapter 4** for more detail).

Table 3.1 above outlines a variety of work-life balance cultural and attitudinal factors that can exist at management and employee levels within an organisation. Depending on the work-life balance strategy that is deemed most suitable and desirable by the organisation, certain cultural and attitudinal issues need to be present to ensure a fit between the WLB strategy and the WLB culture at employee and management level. If there is a mismatch, it will prove difficult to achieve the work-life balance strategy. It is also critical that these attitudes and work-life balance cultural assumptions are shared by all key stakeholders, including senior management, middle / line management, and employees. **Panel 3.1** below draws on the findings of the *2007 Work-Life Balance in Ireland* study in relation to alignment of WLB attitudes among HR directors / managers, middle / line managers, and employees.

Panel 3.1: Aligning Work-Life Balance Attitudes

To gauge the attitudes of the various stakeholders towards work-life balance, the following are some of the issues that should be explored:

- Attitudes towards working patterns and impact on the business.
- Perceptions regarding the duties and responsibilities of the employer / organisation.
- Expectations regarding the right to balance work and personal life domains.
- Attitudes towards impact of work-life balance for employees.
- Perceived fairness of work-life balance programme availability.

Source: 2007 Work-Life Balance in Ireland *study.*

The attitudes of HR directors / managers, middle / line managers and employees towards work-life balance were explored in the *2007 Work-Life Balance in Ireland* study. **Table 3.2** presents the findings for the percentage of respondents agreeing or disagreeing with a number of statements regarding work-life balance attitudes and perceptions.

The data in this study shows that differences exist across the various levels in organisations in relation to attitudes and work-life balance culture issues. Generally, management and employees share similar attitudes regarding the employers' duties and responsibilities as well as the positive impact work-life balance has on employee well-being. HR directors tend to disagree more than line managers and employees with the statement that work-life balance policies and practices can be perceived to be unfair to some employees (for example, those without childcare or eldercare duties).

Table 3.2: Work-Life Balance Culture & Attitude Statements – Multi-Stakeholder Comparison

WLB Culture & Attitude Statement	HR directors/ managers		Middle / line managers		Employees	
	Agree	Disagree	Agree	Disagree	Agree	Disagree
Employees must not expect to change working patterns if to do so would disrupt the business.	80%	20%	74%	26%	41%	59%
The employer's first responsibility is to ensure it achieves its goals.	100%	0%	94%	6%	90%	10%
Everyone should be able to balance their work and home lives.	60%	40%	55%	45%	91%	9%
It is not the organisation's responsibility to help people balance their work and life.	0%	100%	19%	81%	29%	71%
People work best when they can balance work and other aspects of their lives.	100%	0%	99%	1%	97%	3%
Policies for staff to balance work / life are often unfair to some employees.	27%	73%	59%	41%	48%	52%

Source: 2007 Work-Life Balance in Ireland *study.*

Organisations can assess the attitudes and work-life balance cultural perceptions that prevail by exploring the issues set out in **Table 3.2**. It is important that there is alignment in attitudes and perceptions from senior management to middle / line management to employee level if work-life balance strategy is to be effectively achieved.

Step 2: Develop a Work-Life Balance Strategy

A clear strategy on work-life balance is required if an organisation is to design and implement work-life balance policies and practices effectively.[31] This strategy should be clearly articulated, accessible to all management and staff, and communicated effectively to ensure a common understanding. WLB strategy statements represent the overarching organisation philosophy regarding employee work-life balance. The strategy should be designed in line with the culture of the business, the reality of business needs, as well as the needs of employees and management. The strategy determines the overall work-life balance ethos within the organisation.

Work-life balance strategy in organisations can range from being non-existent at one end of the continuum to being well-embedded into organisational life through the implementation and management of various work-life balance policies and practices available to a large cohort of staff. Research undertaken by the Work-Life Balance Network in Ireland in 2004 sets out a diagnostic framework for organisations to establish how advanced their organisation is in terms of work-life balance strategy and practice.[32] The

---

[31]   Parasuraman & Greenhaus (1999).
[32]   Work-Life Balance Network (2004).

report presents a four-stage model for moving from an undeveloped, or underdeveloped, approach to work-life balance to a mature approach:

- **Stage 1 – Formative:** At this stage, the organisation is not very focused on work-life balance issues and the attitude, culture and work-life balance strategy is quite rudimentary. The general perception is that employees do not face issues in managing the worlds of work and family life and, if they do, such problems are not of concern to the organisation. The need for work-life balance policies is not acknowledged, since employees are believed to be able to separate the worlds of work and personal life.

- **Stage 2 – Broadening:** Organisations whose approach to work-life balance is representative of this stage tend to take more of a pro-active approach to work-life balance, providing some work-life balance and flexible working practices. However, work-life balance for organisations at this stage tends to be seen as a female issue and uptake of initiatives can be quite low.

- **Stage 3 – Deepening:** Organisations operating at this level address cultural issues and engage with work-life balance in a more strategic manner. Work-life balance is a HR issue that receives attention in HR policy and practice.

- **Stage 4 – Mature:** This is the most advanced work-life balance design and implementation strategy in organisations. Work-life balance policies and practices are in place to meet the needs of the organisation, as well as the employees. Such policies and practices are embedded into the everyday life of the business and are monitored and evaluated to ensure their effectiveness.

The approach organisations take to work-life balance can be assessed against the four-stage framework above to determine where their work-life balance strategy falls along the continuum. Evidence from Canada presents a work-life balance strategy development continuum,[33] similar in nature to the diagnostic model presented below (see **Figure 3.2**).

This continuum can act as:

- An evaluation tool to establish where the organisation currently is placed in terms of its work-life balance strategy.

- A planning tool to assist an organisation to establish what needs to be put in place to move along the continuum.

The continuum proposes that organisations can assess their progress, from being inactive in terms of work-life balance strategy, policy and practice (formative) to being very interactive and advanced (mature) in their work-life balance policies and practice.

As an organisation progresses along the continuum from left to right, a variety of differences are evident in terms of the characteristics or features of work-life balance strategy in the organisation (as listed in the first column). For example, the focus on employees' families at the inactive level is proposed to be family-forgetful, as opposed to employees' families being a central focus of concern in organisations that present an interactive and embedded work-life strategy. Organisations need to analyse and evaluate what level of maturity they require from their work-life balance strategy to suit their organisational, business, and employee needs.

---

[33] HRSDC (2005).

Figure 3.2: The Work-Life Strategy Development Continuum

	Inactive	Re-active	Active	Pro-active	Interactive
Family	Family-forgetful	Family-aware	Family-friendly	Family-supportive	Family-advocate
Approach	None	Some programmatic policies	Organisational level	Cultural change	Integrated
Perception	Personal issue	Women's issue	Competitive issue	Economic issue	Social & economic issue
Responsibilities	Work responsibilities	Child-care needs	Life-cycle & personal responsibilities	Shared responsibility	Collective responsibility
Action	None	Some informal investigation research	Employee surveys & opinions	Influential research; impact assessments	Applied collaborative research
Focus	Work & family segregation	Work & family interference; role overload	Work & family balance	Work & life integration	Work, family, life harmony

Source: Adapted from Human Resource & Social Development Canada (2005).

The level of maturity of the work-life balance strategy statements varied greatly from one organisation to the other depending on a variety of factors including:

- **Senior management attitude towards WLB**: Organisations with supportive senior managers usually have work-life balance as a central HR management policy.

- **The nature of the business:** It can be more challenging for certain types of businesses to adopt certain work-life balance policies (for example, manufacturing) and, thus, the work-life balance strategy can be more limited in scope, due to business needs.

- **Number of employees:** The SME sector tends to offer fewer formal work-life balance initiatives than larger organisations. However, some SMEs operate more informal and flexible practices that are agreed on a one-to-one basis between the employer and employee.

- **Past experience with WLB policies and practices:** Organisations with more experience in implementing and managing various work-life balance programmes tend to have a clear work-life balance strategy statement compared with organisations that have less WLB experience.

- **Private *versus* public sector:** The public sector tends to have work-life balance as a key HR strategy, emphasising the right for employees to avail of more reduced working hours practices than the private sector.

- **Employee demand:** The demand for flexible working practices or work-life balance practices from employees will influence WLB strategy. Organisations whose employees have greater demand for work-life balance initiatives usually have a more integrated work-life balance strategy compared with organisations where employees present fewer demands.

The work-life balance strategy statement should refer to the rationale for work-life balance in the organisation and its overall aims and objectives. **Table 3.3** sets out examples of WLB statements from various public and private sector organisations in Ireland.

Table 3.3: Sample Work-Life Balance Strategy Statements

Organisation	Statement
AIB	"AIB Bank recognises that staff may require flexibility in their work patterns at certain times in their career, when balancing varying priorities between their personal and working lives."
Bank of Ireland	"In pursuing our business objectives, we will have due regard to each individual's need to fulfil family / personal commitments. We will seek to support and assist employees in a willing and flexible manner when their personal circumstances require it."
Civil & Public Service	"Priority will be given to putting in place enhanced policies to support families in a changing society and, in particular, to ensure that policies are designed to promote family formation and family life."
ESB	"Flexibility in the workplace enables each individual to combine their working career with family life and other commitments and thus assist them in reaching their full potential as valued employees."
Hewlett-Packard	"We have affirmed our intent to help employees develop work / life skills and to provide tools, resources and a supportive environment to assist in work / life navigation."
IBM Ireland	"It is in our best interest to help employees balance the pressures of work with the demands of home. Through work / life programmes, employees have greater access to the workplace and are more productive because their personal issues can be easily addressed."
Intel	"Intel is committed to providing tools and work environment solutions that reduce barriers to effectiveness caused by work and personal life challenges, maximizing employee contributions over the course of their careers, and enhancing Intel's Great Place To Work value."
UCD	"UCD sees the promotion of flexible working arrangements and work-life balance initiatives as vital to achieving a productive, healthy workplace. We see each staff member as an individual with unique requirements and needs."

Source: Taken from various organisation websites and published organisation documentation.

The following are some of the key features of these work-life balance statements:

- Assisting employees to balance work and personal life demands and domains.
- The provision of arrangements / tools to assist employees to manage work and life better.
- Supportive work-life balance working environment.
- Acknowledgement that employees are valued in the business.
- Reference to the expected outcomes and consequences of focusing on work-life balance (more productive workforce, greater flexibility, and supporting family life).

It is important that the organisation decides what its needs and requirements are from a business, management, and employee perspective. Understanding these requirements should dictate the work-life balance strategy appropriate to the particular organisation. A best-fit approach is deemed most suitable, which means that the organisation, following thorough multi-level investigation of needs and requirements, adopts a work-life balance strategy, policies and practices that will work well for the organisation. In some cases, a less sophisticated or immature work-life balance strategy might be deemed suitable but, in other cases, a more advanced work-life balance strategy and approach may be necessary, given demands from employees. The model proposed in this book will assist organisations in determining the most appropriate WLB strategy and approach for their business.

Thus, in developing a work-life balance strategy statement, the following questions should be asked:

- What is the overall objective of WLB policy and practice for the organisation?
- What are the benefits to be achieved for the business, for management, and for employees of work-life balance policies and practices?
- Why focus on work-life balance as a HR issue?

Step 3: Determine Employees' Work-Life Balance Needs & Requirements

The third stage in designing work-life balance policies and programmes is an assessment of employee needs and demands. It is important to establish clearly what issues employees face to ensure that the subsequent programmes and arrangements offered are an appropriate match to employee needs. A number of options are available to determine employee WLB needs, including workplace surveys and focus groups consisting of representative groups from various organisational sectors. Step 4 below focuses on the importance of including multiple stakeholders in the design and implementation of work-life balance policies and programmes.

In the past, many organisations have focused more on family-friendly working arrangements geared towards employees with childcare responsibilities. However, it is important to consider all employees in the work-life balance design process, irrespective of caring duties. The needs of employees in relation to balancing work, family and lifestyle commitments can be ascertained through a variety of mechanisms:

- Asking employees individually (this may work best in small workplaces).
- Open discussion with employees in staff meetings or through employee representative groups.
- Conducting focus groups.
- Asking employees through employee surveys or including WLB questions in an employee attitude survey.
- Seeking managers and supervisors' input.
- Conducting a formal work-life balance survey.

The most effective method of assessing employee work-life balance needs is a combination of the methods listed above. It is important to gather information for all groups of employees working across different sectors and units in the organisation. A work-life balance questionnaire distributed to all staff is an effective means of gathering data of relevance to all employees. This data then could be explored further by conducting a number of focus group sessions with certain cohorts of staff to gather further information or seek clarification on the data gathered. **Table 3.4** below sets out some key questions that should be included in an employee questionnaire / survey, when exploring employee work-life balance needs and preferences.

Table 3.4: Determining Employees' Work-Life Balance Needs –
Questionnaire / Survey Items

Topic/Issue	Objective	Indicative Questions
Preferences for particular WLB programmes	To identify which programmes would be most suitable from an employee perspective.	Identify and rank which programmes, policies, and practices would be most useful in helping employees achieve greater work-life balance: job-sharing; part-time working; flexi-time; term-time working; home working / tele-working; time off in lieu; annualised hours; paternity leave; informal flexibility / emergency leave; compressed working week; employee counselling and support; career breaks; education schemes; on-site / off-site medical facilities / doctor / nurse; membership / discounts at gym, shops, etc; on-site crèche; subsidised nursery places outside work; financial advisors; others?
Current work-life balance	To evaluate the current employee work-life balance state.	Does your job keeps you away too much from the people and activities that are important to you? Do you feel you have more to do that you can handle comfortably? Do you wish you had more time to do things for yourself? Do you feel physically drained when you get home from work? Do you feel you have to rush to get everything done each day?
Work demands	To assess the current demands on employee time.	Do you regularly bring work home at weekends? Do you continue working after your colleagues have gone home? Do you have enough time to stay on a consistent exercise programme? Do you regularly find yourself thinking about work when you are engaged in non-work activities?
Perceptions of managerial support for WLB	To evaluate how supportive managers are of work-life balance.	In general, are managers in this organisation accommodating of personal needs? Do senior management in this organisation encourage supervisors / line managers to be sensitive to employees' personal / non-work concerns? Are middle managers and supervisors in this organisation sympathetic toward employees' child-care and other commitments outside work? Are middle managers and supervisors in this organisation sympathetic towards employees' elder-care responsibilities? In the event of conflict, are managers and supervisors understanding when employees have to put their personal / non-work lives first?
Work-life balance culture and support	To assess the WLB culture in the organisation.	Does this organisation have relevant programmes and policies designed to help employees balance work and personal / non-work life? Does this organisation make an active effort to help employees when there is a conflict between work and personal / non-work life? Is it easy to find out about work-life balance support programmes in this organisation? Is this organisation supportive when an employee wants to switch to a less demanding job for personal reasons? Does this organisation respect your desire to balance work and personal / non-work demands?

Source: Adapted from the 2007 Work-Life Balance in Ireland *study.*

Focus groups are a useful means of exploring employee WLB needs and requirements. **Table 3.5** sets out some of the topics for potential discussion in such groups. The focus groups should include representatives from all sections of the organisation, as well as managers at different levels. The greater the diversity in the focus group, the more rounded and informed the discussion should be.

**Table 3.5: Determining Employees' Work-Life Balance Needs –
Focus Group Topics**

Topic / Issue	Objective	Indicative Questions
General	To assess general WLB attitudes and issues.	What do you think this organisation does well in assisting staff get a satisfactory work-life balance? Which are most important? What does this organisation do that makes it harder for staff to get a satisfactory work-life balance? Which have the most impact?
Expectations	To evaluate WLB expectations.	When you started your job, did you know what to expect about working rosters, shifts, hours? If so, how did you know? If not, would it have been useful to know? What would have been the best way for this organisation to do that?
Awareness and understanding of existing WLB programmes	To assess the level of awareness of existing WLB policy & practice.	Does this organisation currently have a written work-life balance policy? If yes, do you think it is easy to understand how this policy can be used to assist staff to balance their work and personal responsibilities? Are you familiar with the processes involved in taking up current flexible work / work-life balance arrangements? Do you know where you would go to find out more about flexible work and family options within this organisation?
Support from your line manager	To evaluate how supportive managers are of work-life balance.	Does your manager help or hinder you in getting a satisfactory work-life balance? What do they do? Is there anything you think would be useful for them to do differently? How comfortable are you talking to your manager about work-life issues? What helps? What makes it harder?
Preferences for particular WLB programmes	To identify which programmes would be most suitable.	Discussion of the advantages and disadvantages of a range of work-life balance policies and practices including: job-sharing; part-time working; flexi-time; term-time working; home working / tele-working; time off in lieu; annualised hours; paternity leave; informal flexibility / emergency leave; compressed working week; employee counselling and support; career breaks; education schemes; on-site / off-site medical facilities / doctor / nurse; membership / discounts at gym, shops, etc; on-site crèche; subsidised nursery places outside work; financial advisors; others?

*Source: Taken from various sources, including the Department of Labour, New Zealand
(http://www.dol.govt.nz/worklife/index.asp) and Hudson Highland Group (2005).*

Step 4: Consultation & Communication Process

Step 4 is the consultation and communication process for managing WLB policies and practices, which is intended to help organisations to establish direct and representative arrangements for informing and consulting effectively with staff in the design, implementation and evaluation of WLB initiatives. It aims to support HR practitioners who are dealing with a range of challenges in informing and consulting with their stakeholders (employees, managers and employee forum / union representatives) and considers many of the key issues, while suggesting possible approaches to ensure the successful implementation of WLB initiatives.

Consultation & Communication

Consultation is defined in the regulations[34] as the "exchange of views and establishment of a dialogue between the employer and information and consultation representatives". The purpose of consultation and communication is to ensure that all stakeholders in the WLB process are involved and have an opportunity to contribute towards the design and formation of WLB policies and practices, which can ensure greater buy-in and joint ownership of the strategy and individual elements contained therein.

One of the key messages in this section is that informing and consulting with employees is an evolutionary process. There are very few organisations that can set up consultation and communication arrangements and expect them to operate effectively from the outset. What is key, however, is that not consulting and communicating with the relevant stakeholders is inappropriate. The success rate of any WLB initiative or strategy is greatly enhanced through the use of an appropriate consultation and communication process.

WLB initiatives should be an integral part of the overall business plan. Designing and developing an effective WLB strategy is only the beginning of the process; it then needs to be operationalised. In order to ensure a smooth transition from designing and developing to operating any WLB strategy, it is essential that a consultation and communication process is put in place, linked to that strategy. The purpose of the process is to ensure that all the key stakeholders are clear about their role in making the WLB strategy and its various initiatives a reality. Consultation and communication is also about reinforcing the key messages and consistency in the regular flow of information between stakeholders, thereby building trust between the parties.

WLB initiatives, as we have seen in **Chapter 2**, can play an integral part in the successful achievement of an organisation's business goals. However, in order for any initiative to be successful, it requires all the stakeholders in the process to be involved from the outset. Consultation and communication play a key role in ensuring that this happens and the level of consultation and communication is dependent on the company's current stage of the WLB evolution. The stages of evolution of the consultation and communication process are set out in **Table 3.6**.

---

[34]   Employees (Provision of Information & Consultation) Act 2006.

Table 3.6: Consultation & Communication Process for Work-Life Balance Initiatives at Different Stages of Work-Life Balance Evolution

Stage	Characteristics	Evidence	
Formative	Communications are formal, through authorised circulars or through strict managerial lines. Information is shared on a need-to-know basis.	Staff meetings are briefing sessions. Staff issues are raised through representatives. Staff opinions are not sought, either formally or informally. Personnel information is held only by the HR department.	
Broadening	Communications are formal through authorised circulars or through strict managerial lines. General information on organisation goals is shared. Information is not generally available in user-friendly format.	Staff meetings are briefing sessions. Staff issues are raised through representatives. Staff opinions are sought by some managers on an informal basis. Some managers hold information on personnel policies and processes. Generally, policy information is circulated but not refreshed or promoted.	
Deepening	Formal consultation and communication processes are supported by information meetings with questions and answers Consultation and communications is a two-way process, driven by management and employees.	Staff opinions are pro-actively sought by managers and through formal surveys. Communication of the organisation's business strategy and objectives happens annually through a formal communication process. Employee forum / union representatives are involved in the consultation meetings.	
Mature	Consultation & communication is seen as the lifeblood of the organisation. Middle / line managers are seen as critical information sources. Multiple communication channels are used. Effectiveness of consultation and communication is monitored and evaluated.	Regular team exchange meetings with open and meaningful dialogue (briefings, focus groups) take place. Staff opinions are pro-actively sought by managers and through focus groups and formal surveys. Information is cascaded up, as well as down. Information on policies, procedures, etc. are readily available to all staff. Effective communication is included in management core competencies and development plans.	

Source: Adapted from Work-Life Balance Network (2004).

Who are the Work-Life Balance Stakeholders?

Given the importance of communication and consultation of WLB policies and practices, it is important to establish who must be communicated and consulted with within the organisation. The various WLB stakeholders in an organisation are presented in **Figure 3.3**.

Figure 3.3: Work-Life Balance Stakeholders

The Work Foundation[35] survey found that the top four objectives of internal communication activities, as stated by organisations, are:

- Engaging employees in achieving business objectives.
- Understanding of organisational goals and strategy.
- Supporting culture change.
- Creating an environment of open dialogue across the organisation.

Creating an environment of open dialogue across the organisation is significant, because it shows that communication in organisations today is not simply a top-down approach. The more progressive organisations look for a two-way communication process. When a good two-way communication process exists, it can help to build the psychological contract, in which employees feel valued by their employer and feel that their inputs are seen as valuable to the success of the business. According to CIPD research,[36] the two central elements to achieving employee engagement are ensuring that:

- Employees have the opportunity to give upward feedback.
- Employees feel well-informed about what is happening in their organisation.

Thus, better work-life balance programme design and implementation should result from consulting with the various stakeholders who will be affected by the WLB initiatives.

The real challenge for organisations, in terms of consultation, is managing employee expectations. If employees are asked for feedback or input on WLB policy, and their feedback is not acted upon, it can have a negative effect on the relationship and trust

---

[35]   Bingham & Cuff (2002).
[36]   CIPD (2006a).

between management and employees. Therefore, when organisations are consulting and communicating in a meaningful way with their employees, it is advisable to set the parameters from the outset, ensuring that the rules of the consultation and communication process are understood and thereby minimising the likelihood of adverse reactions.

Implicit in this process is that managers, and in particular middle / line managers, play a central role in any WLB consultation and communication strategy. The efforts of the senior management team can be negated and mutual trust damaged by middle / line managers who fail to deliver or misrepresent WLB policy information. Equally, there is real and significant danger should they fail to convey the feedback given by their employees to the senior management team and HR. Therefore, middle / line manager involvement in the design and formation of work-life balance initiatives is believed to be an important predictor of their attitude towards these programmes, which in turn determines WLB success or failure.[37]

Methods of Consultation & Communication

The consultation and communication process for each organisation is dependent on the stage of WLB evolution and the overall WLB strategy adopted. Consultation can take various formats and information can be delivered through a variety of channels. Some employees prefer to have the message delivered verbally, whereas others pay greater attention when the message is delivered in writing or electronically. If the WLB message is important, it may be necessary to deliver it more than once and in more than one way. If organisations want to change attitudes towards WLB, it may be necessary to examine ways to reinforce key messages continually. The more ways in which this can be done (through example by senior management and by highlighting successful case studies, for example), the more likely the WLB strategy will be received successfully, allowing for maximum benefits to be accrued.

The developments in technology, most notably web-based technologies, have increased the range of options for effective communication. In many organisations, intranet and email-based communication are now more relevant than traditional methods, like printed newsletters. One of the benefits of electronically-transmitted information is immediacy, thus enabling instant feedback. However, it is important that organisations choose a method (or methods) of communication that can reach all stakeholders and employees – for example, shop-floor employees or drivers may not have access to intranet or email. Furthermore, evaluating the effectiveness of the WLB initiatives for the individuals and demonstrating 'value' to the organisation can be carried out through web-based questionnaires, email surveys and online forums.

Table 3.7 outlines a number of methods of consultation and communication, which may be used when designing, implementing and evaluating WLB initiatives. The table also outlines the relevance and potential value of each approach, together with the potential challenges when using each approach.

---

[37] McCarthy, Grady & Darcy (2007).

Table 3.7: Approaches to Effective Consultation & Communication

Approach to consultation & communication	Relevance & value of the approach	Challenges in using this approach
Attitude Surveys	Employee attitude surveys are a useful way in which employers can obtain quantitative feedback on WLB initiatives as to employee needs, ease of access to WLB programmes, and the effectiveness of existing initiatives.	Designing the survey: ensuring that the 'right' questions are asked will determine the success of this approach. A poorly-designed attitudinal survey can lead to incorrect perceptions and information.
Focus groups	Focus groups are an effective way to obtain qualitative feedback on WLB initiatives, on employee needs, ease of access and effectiveness of the existing programmes from all the relevant stakeholders.	It is essential to involve the relevant stakeholders in the group. It is important not to raise expectations that cannot be met. Groups need to be structured so that the views of all the stakeholders are taken into account.
Face-to-face discussions with managers	Employees can express their views directly to middle / line managers. This potentially can be an effective method of two-way feedback. Information as to employee needs, how the WLB initiatives will work / are working, and employee satisfaction with WLB initiatives they have availed of, can be gathered.	Managers need to understand the importance of upward feedback and the consistency of their behaviour will determine the success of this approach. Equally, employees may feel inhibited in discussing openly their views, if they perceive that doing so could affect their career prospects adversely.
Team briefings / group meetings	Information on WLB initiatives can be delivered by middle / line managers to established work teams / groups. By using smaller group / team and face-to-face communication, more effective dialogue is possible, hence more useful feedback is gathered.	Ensuring consistency in the message delivered by different managers is a challenge. If managers are transmitting the same message, they may deliver it somewhat differently with different emphases, which can lead to misunderstanding for employees.
Staff presentations	Presentations delivered by senior management can be powerful. This approach can be useful to present the WLB strategy to be adopted by the organisation or to outline already designed policies and programmes and how they can be implemented effectively.	This approach is dependent on the communication skills of the manager and the method of presentation. Time should be allowed for questions and answers. This is not considered to be a full two-way communication process because many employees may feel inhibited in having a full and frank discussion in an open forum type situation. Consideration should be given to non-native English speakers where scope for misunderstanding may increase.

Approach to consultation & communication	Relevance & value of the approach	Challenges in using this approach
Emails & Intranets	Messages via email can be targeted to particular groups such as middle / line managers to communicate the policies and programmes for implementation. Feedback facilities can be incorporated in intranets, so there is some opportunity for two-way communication. Employee attitude surveys as discussed above can be conducted by email.	Intranet and email are not always available to all staff and alternative methods of communication must be considered to ensure all staff members receive the same communication.
Video & in-house TV	This approach is useful in particular in larger organisations for introducing policies and programmes. This form of communication is mainly passive.	If organisations use this approach to communication, they should ensure the video is well-produced and relevant. This method of communication is expensive and does not gather employee feedback.
Letters	Addressed to individuals and possibly sent to their homes. This form of communication is often used for issues of major importance.	Not very appropriate for design, implementation and evaluation of WLB initiatives, since employee feedback and input cannot be gathered. May be useful in conjunction with other methods.
Newsletters / In-house magazines	Produced on a monthly or bi-monthly basis and may carry features on organisational news. Can be used to promote WLB programmes, features on new initiatives being launched or successful case studies.	They can play a role in integrated communication of policies and programmes but not certain that all staff will read them. This approach needs to be used in combination with other methods of communication.
Notices / Bulletin boards	Can be considered a traditional method of communication. Can be used to advertise WLB Day and the programme of events, in combination with other methods of communication.	Not recommended for important announcements.

Source: Adapted from CIPD (2007b).

Chapter Summary

This chapter set out what organisations should do at the four stages involved in work-life balance strategy, policy, and programme design.

The importance of determining the overall work-life balance strategy was highlighted and some diagnostic frameworks presented on how to advance the work-life balance strategy.

Sample work-life balance strategy statements from a range of organisations were presented.

The importance of establishing the constraints of the business context is critical to ensure that work-life balance strategy, policy and practice is designed and implemented within the reality of the business context. The culture that prevails in the organisation, at all levels from senior management to the employee level, is an important determinant of work-life balance effectiveness.

A multi-stakeholder approach should be adopted during the design stage incorporating input from senior management, HR management, middle / line management, and employees to establish work-life balance needs and requirements thus allowing the design of WLB policies and programmes aligned to these needs.

Finally, a comprehensive consultation and communication process is necessary to gain buy-in from the relevant stakeholders.

*Once the work-life balance strategy, policy and practices have been designed, the implementation of these becomes critical and **Chapter 4** discusses what organisations can do to implement work-life balance policies and practices effectively.*

4: Implementing WLB Policies & Programmes

"Implementing work-life balance policies and programmes sends a positive message to employees that there is an option for flexibility and that the organisation is caring towards its employees."
— *Middle / line manager,* **2007 Work-Life Balance in Ireland** *study* **participant, Private sector**

This chapter sets out how organisations can move from the rhetoric surrounding work-life balance to the reality of effective implementation of policies that enable both organisations and employees to gain benefits from WLB initiatives.

The chapter begins by setting out what organisations should do to establish which types of policies and programmes are most suitable to their organisation. Consequently, it deals with steps 5 to 7 of the best practice implementation model as set out in **Chapter 1**.

A planned and systematic procedure is outlined, which sets out the stages that the employer and employee should carry out for successful implementation of these policies.

Finally, training for implementation is discussed.

Sample forms for best practice implementation are included in **Appendix B**.

WLB Implementation: Towards A Holistic Approach

Once the work-life balance strategy has been considered and the needs of the employees established, WLB practices and programmes need to be developed in line with the business needs. The first important step towards implementation is choosing which programmes are most suitable to the organisation (step 5).

Figure 4.1: Implementing Work-Life Balance Policies & Programmes

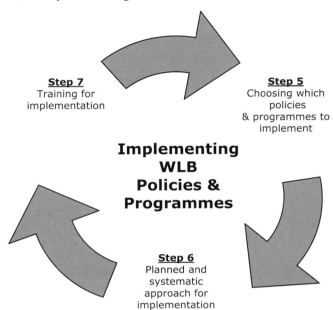

Step 5: Choose the Types of WLB/Flexible Practices to Adopt

A wide variety of work-life balance or flexible working arrangements and practices are available to organisations. This section briefly describes these practices and **Table 4.1** summarises the key features, advantages and disadvantages associated with each arrangement.

It is apparent from **Table 4.1** that a wide variety of work-life balance options are available to organisations. Organisations must decide which initiatives and practices are most suitable, by exploring their WLB strategy, employee needs, and business needs. The following case studies demonstrate how four different organisations have designed and implemented work-life balance practices tailored to their needs and requirements:

- **Case study 4.1** explains how the Revenue Commissioners are introducing a pilot e-working initiative.

- **Case study 4.2** details the 'Camp Kool' WLB initiative in operation in Intel Ireland.

- **Case study 4.3** presents how Life-Balance Time operates as an alternative to term-time working in the ESB.

- **Case Study 4.4** discusses how Medtronic has designed, and is implementing, a pilot flexi-time programme called 'MyTime'.

Table 4.1: Summary of Work-Life Balance / Flexible Working Practices

WLB / Flexible working practice	Key features	Advantages	Disadvantages / Challenges
Job-sharing	Reduced working hours. A full-time job shared by two or more employees, with salary and benefits also shared.	Allows for continuity in key posts. Effective reduced working hours policy.	Need job-share partner. Communication and co-ordination between job-sharers essential. The headcount is considered to be the same as full-time worker but line managers only have a 50% contribution from each job-sharer.
Part-time working	Reduced working hours. A system of working fewer than the standard full-time hours.	Can be used to retain skilled employees who want to work fewer hours. Flexibility for the organisation and the employee.	Reduction in working hours, so employee's non-working hours need to be covered by other staff. Pro-rata reduction in benefits and salary for employees. The headcount is considered to be the same as full-time worker but line managers only have a reduced contribution from each part-time worker.
Flexi-time	A system where employees can vary start and finish times around a set of core hours. Adapted to personal and business needs.	Employees can vary working times to suit personal responsibilities. No impact on actual number of hours worked. Can deliver flexibility for the business where more employees work during busier periods.	Ensure adequate cover during all hours of business / operation. Time and attendance systems to ensure employees are working the necessary hours.
Term-time	Unpaid leave during school holidays for employees with school-going childcare responsibilities. Usually only available to those with childcare responsibilities.	Gives employees time off for extra childcare responsibilities over the summer. Greater employee flexibility.	Administration and management of cover for those on leave. Can be perceived to be unfair to those employees without school-going childcare responsibilities.
Life-balance time	Period of leave available to all employees for a certain length of time (6 to 20 weeks). Employees can use this initiative to facilitate needs for personal development, education, travel, childcare, time-out and preparing for retirement.	Gives all employees an opportunity for time off to support their various needs. Seen to be fair and equitable to all employees, compared to term-time working which applies only to employees with childcare responsibilities.	Administration and management of replacement staff for employees availing of this initiative.

WLB / Flexible working practice	Key features	Advantages	Disadvantages / Challenges
E-working / Tele-working	Employees work all or some of the time at home or working from home as a base. Requires good ICT infrastructure and facilities.	Fewer commuting problems. Allows employees more time to balance their work and home lives.	Managing employees from a distance. Social issues for employees who work exclusively from home (feeling isolated). Only suitable for certain jobs.
Time off in lieu	Time off for extra hours worked above contracted employment hours.	Employees can work up extra time to enable time off when required. Flexibility to take time off without taking from annual leave.	Time and attendance administration and management more challenging. Must ensure adequate cover at all times. Business planning can be more uncertain and difficult.
Annualised hours	An agreed number of hours worked over the year with the weekly hours being 'flexed' to meet fluctuations in service demands.	Flexibility for the employee and employer around personal or business needs respectively.	Managing cover during anti-social working times and periods can be difficult to negotiate.
Paternity leave	A set period off work for the father at the time of the birth of his child (for example, three days). Not a statutory entitlement in Ireland.	Recognises the importance of family life. Gives the father time off without impacting on annual leave at the time of the birth of his child.	May be perceived to be unfair among male employees who do not have children.
Compressed working week / condensed working hours	Carrying out a full-time job in less than five working days per week – for example, over four days.	Greater flexibility for the employee. Greater flexibility for the organisation to organise extra working time around business needs, where possible.	Longer working days need to be in line with working time legislation (for example, Organisation of Working Time Act).
Employee counselling and support	Counselling and support for parenting and personal issues, commonly provided through employee assistance programmes.	Recognises the importance of family and personal life in the workplace. Free to the employee as the cost is usually borne by the employer.	Can be costly for the employer.
Career breaks	Extended period of leave from work (unpaid), with agreed date of return to work.	Gives employee flexibility to travel, study etc., without having to resign from job.	Possible requirement to up-skill employee on return to work.
On-site / off-site medical facilities / doctor / nurse	Doctor / nurse facilities on-site perhaps certain times during the week.	Convenient for employee and cost usually borne by employer.	Can be costly for the employer.
Membership / discounts (gym, shops)	Free or discounted membership to gyms, social clubs, etc.	Can assist employees in managing work and recreation and can have positive motivational impact.	Can be costly for the employer.

CASE STUDY 4.1

The Revenue Commissioners

Pilot Study on e-Working

Michelle Carroll, HR Strategy Manager at the Revenue Commissioners, explains the Revenue's experience with an e-working pilot scheme.

Q: What was the overall objective of the work-life balance policy / project?

A: The Programme for Prosperity and Fairness (PPF) contained a Government commitment to introduce e-working arrangements into the Public Service. Following on from this commitment, Revenue introduced a pilot e-working scheme for one year in late 2007. The overall objective of the pilot is to assist staff in achieving a greater work-life balance, while allowing the organisation to gain from the anticipated benefits arising from e-working, such as increased retention of staff, employer of choice, reduced absenteeism, increased job satisfaction, etc.

Q: What was involved in the project?

A: Piloting e-working was researched by a sub-committee of Revenue's Human Resources Partnership Group, who prepared and issued a report in May 2002. This committee's overall recommendation was that Revenue should develop a pilot scheme built around a formal e-working model i.e. predominantly home-working.

Following this review, a cross-divisional project team was established to further examine the topic with particular emphasis on the costs, savings and benefits involved. The team also examined the challenges in introducing an e-working option within Revenue. The project team concurred with the thinking of the original group in favouring a formal e-working scheme i.e. four days home working with mandatory attendance in the office on the fifth day.

Consultations were held with two sections of the Department to identify the costs associated with introducing an e-working pilot. The estimated initial set-up costs included the funding of the following: Secure ID, Licences, Broadband connection and annual rental, PC, Office furniture, etc.

Three areas within the Revenue Commissioners agreed to participate in a pilot e-working programme. It was considered particularly important for the pilot scheme that the work determined suitable would be easy to measure and quantify.

Following consultation with the Board of the Revenue Commissioners, it was decided that a pilot e-working scheme should be put in place consisting of the following elements:

- A 12-month pilot scheme commencing in Quarter 4, 2007.
- 80% home working – four days a week, with mandatory attendance in the office on the fifth day.
- A pilot scheme available to 50 people in the regions / divisions taking part.
- The scheme may not be combined with any other Work-Life Balance scheme.
- No guarantee for individuals selected for the pilot that they can continue to e-work beyond the life-time of the pilot.
- No guarantee that the pilot will be continued/extending beyond the initial one-year pilot term.

To be eligible to participate in the e-working pilot, applicants were required to:

- Be serving in an established, full-time capacity.
- Have completed training modules specific to the work involved and have the required experience of the work.
- Be suitable from a health point of view, with particular regard to the provisions of the Dept. of Finance sick leave circulars.
- Be considered suitable for inclusion in the e-working pilot scheme by his/her supervisor and senior management of the Division / Region.
- Have consistently demonstrated personal initiative, commitment and productivity.

As mentioned above, it was initially agreed that there would be 50 participants in the e-working pilot scheme. However, due to the challenges mentioned below, to-date, only 30 people are now involved in the pilot scheme.

Q: What were / are the challenges?

A: The problems included:

1. **ICT problems**: a number of applications had to be declined because the type of secure broadband required by Revenue in order to protect systems and taxpayer information is not available in all areas. It is a precondition of e-working that broadband can be installed in the applicant's home. This was a barrier to involvement in the pilot for a significant number of staff.

2. **Suitable dedicated room**: It is felt that another significant reason for not reaching our quota of 50 was the fact that the jobholder is required to provide a suitable dedicated room to specified dimensions. Not all staff would have such a 'spare' room in their home.

3. **Home insurance policies**: Most home insurance policies are designed specifically for domestic purposes. The e-worker must inform their insurance company of their participation in the scheme to avoid invalidation of their own policies due to undervaluing clauses. Where participants are in rented accommodation, they must ensure that the homeowner informs the insurance company of the change in status.

Q: What did the project deliver – key benefits?

A: As the pilot scheme is in its infancy, it is difficult at this stage to say what key benefits the WLB initiative has actually delivered. Initial evaluations conducted point to increased productivity and higher levels of job satisfaction and motivation.

Q: What evaluation process will be used to determine its success?

A: A series of surveys will be delivered to participants in the e-working pilot, their managers and a colleague representative at various stages throughout the pilot. The Strategic Planning Division will then conduct an in-depth evaluation at the end of the pilot,

taking account of factors such as absenteeism levels, productivity levels, satisfaction levels, etc.

The final evaluation will be conducted by a cross-divisional team that will include involvement by the Organisational Development Unit. The process will identify and report to the Board of the Revenue on:

- The effectiveness of the scheme in meeting business objectives, including an evaluation of productivity and quality of output.

- The actual costs / savings compared to the estimated costs / savings.

- The experience of e-workers.

- Whether the pilot has been a success and recommendations on future courses of action.

- If it is deemed to be a success, what changes / additions should be made to improve its operation and suggestions on the scope of e-working.

Q: Have you received any feedback on the scheme from the various stakeholders?

A: Three months after the commencement of the e-working pilot study, an initial evaluation was carried out.

The results from this survey indicate that e-workers, colleagues and line managers are generally happy with the e-working pilot. A very small percentage of managers felt that the management of e-working staff was more challenging than office-based staff, while the majority of managers felt that e-working resulted in increased productivity.

The main issue raised by both e-workers and their managers was the difficulties with IT. These issues would have to be resolved before consideration could be given to expanding the pilot across the organisation.

– taken from an interview with Michelle Carroll, HR Strategy Manager, Revenue Commissioners.

CASE STUDY 4.2

Intel Ireland:

An Innovative Work-Life Balance Initiative – 'Camp Kool'

Intel Ireland is a major source for the manufacture of high speed Intel® Pentium® 4 microprocessors, support chips and the latest flash memory technology, using leading-edge semiconductor manufacturing processes. It is the centre of manufacturing excellence in Europe and employs approximately 5,500 people. Jacqueline McGrath, HR Generalist, talks about an innovative WLB initiative called 'Camp Kool', which Intel has introduced for its staff.

Q: Is WLB important at Intel?

A: Intel's work-life effectiveness / WLB mission is: "To sustain, introduce and enhance services and programs as appropriate in the organisation to help employees to better manage their busy lives while ensuring organisational success".

In 2001, Intel introduced and enhanced a comprehensive programme of services and working arrangements as appropriate, to help employees to better manage their busy lives, while ensuring organisational success, through three key strategies:

- Introducing an alternative working arrangement policy.

- Developing a childcare strategy for Intel Ireland that would meet the childcare needs of its employees.

- Introducing a number of additional services and programmes across the site.

For the purposes of this case study, the focus is on the Intel Summer Camp initiative known as 'Camp Kool'.

Q: Why was the 'Camp Kool' initiative implemented?

A: In 2001, a review of labour turnover indicators, age profile of site employees and analysis of organisational health surveys identified that many employees were now moving into Stage 2 (family-oriented) of their life-cycle, where significant focus is placed on employees' ability to sustain successful childcare arrangements while at work during the school summer holidays.

Intel recognised that, while summer school holidays can be a joy for children, they can also be a potential headache for parents where normal childcare arrangements are not available for the full period. In response to this trend, and with a strong desire to minimise labour turnover, particularly amongst our female population, the Intel IRL work-life effectiveness team worked on the 'Camp Kool' initiative. The objective was to complement existing childcare provisions to ease the burden on both parents and the business during the summer holiday period.

In 2001, Intel Ireland, in conjunction with Bright Horizons Family Solutions, developed a pilot summer camp for children of Intel employees aged between 5 and 12 years. 'Camp Kool' took place over a four-week period in July of that year and continues now each year. The initial cost was subsidised by Intel. The camp day includes daily lunch, field trips and a 'Camp Kool' t-shirt. During the camp, children participate with children of their own age in a number of activities each day such as sports, arts and crafts, photography, cooking, swimming, orienteering, dance, drama and day trips to many popular centres. The camp times are from 8.00am to 6.00pm, with the aim that, unlike many alternative summer camps, the camp would be in line with the regular working day.

Q: What were / are the challenges?

A: During project design, a number of factors represented key challenges to the team.

1. **Venue:** Considerations here such as parking, proximity to the site and facilities within short walking distances for smaller children were a high priority. On review of a number of possible locations, a suitable venue was acquired at a local National School, just 10 minutes' drive from the Intel site.

2. **Cost:** As the objective of the project was to complement existing childcare arrangements, funding for the project was based on parent contribution, with Intel subsidising this cost. It was imperative that the cost was in line with alternative summer camps and affordable to parents, while the operational cost to the company made the project a feasible and worthwhile initiative.

3. **Numbers**: When the camp was initially advertised, an open and close date for registration was published. However, we have found in recent years, on opening registration, the camp is fully booked very quickly. In response to this, we have continued to expand the number of places available. Since we have limited capacity, as a result of the venue and activities available, demand still far exceeds supply and we have now adopted a first-come, first-served approach.

Q: What does the project deliver – key benefits?
A: The camp is one of the best known initiatives here on the Intel site and one of the key advantages has been to highlight the organisation's commitment to work-life effectiveness / balance. Following the success of the pilot phase in 2001, the camp has grown from strength to strength, increasing in both the number of places available to employees and the number of weeks available.

The organisation has received very positive feedback from employees who previously may have had to take some form of unpaid leave, their statutory holidays or terminate their position because of unsuitable summer childcare arrangements.

Q: How has Intel evaluated the success of this WLB initiative?
A: To determine the level of success of the project, significant emphasis was placed on parent / child feedback and participation rates in the project each year. In 2007, out of 252 questionnaires distributed, 84% rated the camp as 'brilliant'.

Over 91% of parents stated that they would be interested in sending their children to the camp in 2008. In addition, as part of Intel's organisation health strategy, since 2004 employees have been surveyed on a quarterly basis to determine the impact our work-life effectiveness strategies have on the workplace. These results have shown that our work life initiatives are having a positive impact on employee work-life balance, as demonstrated in the graph below.

– taken from an interview with Jacqueline McGrath, HR Generalist, Intel Ireland.

CASE STUDY 4.3

The Electricity Supply Board (ESB):

How Life-Balance Time Operates as an Alternative to Term-Time Working

In 2005, the Electricity Supply Board in Ireland (ESB) launched a work-life balance (WLB) initiative called 'Life-Balance Time'. This was the ESB's response to the WLB initiative known as term-time working, which exists in the public service. The purpose of the Life-Balance Time initiative is to facilitate all employees to achieve a better work-life balance, irrespective of parenting status.

Freida Murray, Equality, Opportunities & Diversity Manager at ESB, said that the issue of term-time working being available only to staff with childcare responsibilities, and not to all staff, was raised in the company by employees. Having consulted with all the relevant stakeholders, the view was that term-time working was more restrictive and could only be of benefit to employees with school-going children. An alternative model, which aimed to be inclusive and would suit the needs of all staff and also meet the business needs of the organisation, was suggested.

Life-Balance Time is a facility for employees to take unpaid leave with agreement from their manager / supervisor. This leave can range from 6 to 20 weeks. The programme enhances the existing menu of work-life balance initiatives that are already available in the organisation. The initiative can be used by employees to facilitate a range of needs, including personal development, education, travel, childcare, time-out and preparing for retirement.

In operating the scheme, long-term planning is required and, once an agreement is reached between the employee and their manager/supervisor, the employee's salary / pay can be spread out evenly over the period of the year that the leave will be taken.

The operational criteria that apply are:

- Continuous service with the organisation.

- Minimum (6 weeks) and maximum (20 weeks) period.

- Agreement between employee and their manager / supervisor.

- Salary / pay, pension / superannuation, annual leave and public holiday adjustments.

The ESB endeavours to facilitate all employee requests to avail of Life-Balance Time during their career; however, certain criteria for selection must be taken into consideration when reviewing applications.

The selection criteria that apply are:

- Operational issues and length of service.

- Flexibility of timing of break (where it suits work patterns).

- Whether an employee is already availing of a flexible work arrangement.

- Whether the employee has availed of Life-Balance Time already.

- Date of request.

- The final decision on each application for request rests with the immediate manager / supervisor and the operation of the scheme is monitored by Human Resources.

Freida says that this WLB initiative is the first of its kind to be introduced in Ireland. She believes that it is beneficial to all staff, in helping them to achieve a balance between work and life. It appeals to the young and old and not just employees who have children. Thus, it is perceived to be more fair and just than traditional term-time leave initiatives, which only cater for a particular cohort of employees - those with school-going children.

– taken from an interview with Freida Murray, Equality, Opportunities & Diversity Manager, ESB.

CASE STUDY 4.4

Medtronic:

Piloting 'MyTime', a Flexi-time System

Medtronic is a global leader in medical technology, developing, manufacturing, selling and supporting a wide variety of products and therapies that alleviate pain, restore health and extend life for millions of people around the world. The company operates worldwide in over 120 countries and employs 2,000 employees in Galway. Dorothy Kelly, HR Director, talks about piloting a flexi-time system that Medtronic has recently introduced for its staff.

Q: Is WLB important at Medtronic?

A: Our workplace has been characterised by continuous change and growing diversity. Flexible work arrangements help employees to achieve a better work-life balance, when combining employment with other responsibilities and choices.

Work-life balance initiatives have benefited the organisation by impacting attraction, retention, absenteeism positively and helping to develop a more productive and engaged workforce, which ultimately supports us in meeting the challenges of today's competitive environment.

Q: Why was flexi-time introduced?

A: At Medtronic, we understand and support the growing need for flexible working arrangements in the workplace and we operate a number of WLB initiatives in our organisation. However, the need for flexi-time was highlighted by a large percentage of employees at Medtronic. There is no doubt that retention of our talented employees was a key influencing factor in developing a flexi-time model.

Consequently, we are presently piloting a flexible working time scheme called 'MyTime' for our Regulatory and Research & Development groups, which impacts approximately 130 employees. The system affords employees greater flexibility in their start / finish times and allows them the flexibility to work up a number of extra days annually.

Q: What was involved in the project?

A: As part of the introduction of the 'MyTime' system, the following best practice process was used:

- The business and employee requirements were reviewed in terms of meeting customer needs, the reality of the workplace, employee satisfaction and ensuring compatibility with relevant legislation.

- Focus groups were held with employees to draft a proposal, which was presented to the management team.

- Meetings were held with managers to obtain their views on how the system could work and input from employees was reviewed.

- Valuable information was obtained from Irish organisations that had already implemented a similar system.

- A pilot period of three months was agreed and success measures were specified.

- Support structures for managers, throughout the implementation stage, were put in place.

- On completion of the pilot period, an evaluation to determine its success was carried out by obtaining the views of employees, management and external customers.

Q: What challenges have you encountered?

A: As with any change initiative, there are many challenges to implementing a flexible working arrangement. However, many of these challenges can be overcome by being mindful of the needs of both the organisation and employees and setting clear ground rules from the outset such as:

- The system must be based primarily on ensuring continuity of support to the business and not for personal reasons

- A comprehensive communication process must be used to ensure employees fully understand the flexi-time system.

- A change of focus among managers with a move away from 'face time' working towards 'results / performance' working must take place.
- Training for Managers to ensure effective implementation

In addition, an accurate time and attendance system was essential, to ensure the efficient running of the 'MyTime' flexible initiative.

Finally, we found that the most significant factor in implementing the flexible work system was to have support from a key member of the leadership team, to act as a powerful champion to drive the project and to promote greater understanding among senior management to ensure buy in.

Q: What did the project deliver – key benefits?

A: As the 'MyTime' flexible initiative is in its infancy, it is difficult to measure its benefits. Initial evaluations conducted found that one of the greatest benefits of the flexible working scheme was the psychological impact for the employee. The knowledge that they can avail of flexibility in their working time has as much a positive impact on employee well-being as exercising the option.

Q: What evaluation process was used to determine its success?

A: The review process was developed and communicated to employees prior to the launch of the pilot scheme. The review process was broken into the following areas:

- Internal and external customers who work closely with the departments were consulted using an email questionnaire.
- Employees were asked to complete an online survey. This was a useful feedback channel to evaluate its success and look at any improvements that could be made.
- Time and attendance reports outlined average hours worked before and during the pilot scheme.

- Using focus groups, managers were asked to review all available data to determine the success of the scheme.
- On completion of the evaluation, the findings were shared with relevant management groups and employees.

Q: Have you received any feedback on the scheme from the various stakeholders?

A: HR Director: "By facilitating a culture of flexible hours, it will help employees reduce commuting times, and create a positive cycle of more efficient and effective work performance. This, in turn, will assist in creating a competitive advantage for Medtronic in attracting and retaining top talent to the organisation. However, flexi-time arrangements require a high degree of commitment and a structured process to monitor the administration aspect."

Middle / line manager: "The benefits of 'MyTime' for the employee include flexibility around start / finish times. Benefits for the company include being able to have employees vary their hours to match fluctuations in demand, positive increases in morale, and retention and attraction."

Employee: "Being a parent, the system allows me a high degree of flexibility in balancing work and home life, which helps me to perform better in my role."

Employee: "The availability of 'MyTime' has allowed me the flexibility to use public transport travelling to and from work. This has been most beneficial for me, as it has reduced stress levels since I am not now working against the clock".

Any flexible working initiative must be managed appropriately to ensure internal equity and its ultimate success. The most advantageous element of piloting the initiative is that you can adjust and improve the system after its implementation to ensure its long-term viability.

- taken from an interview with Dorothy Kelly, HR Director, Medtronic

Choosing the WLB initiatives that are best suited to the organisation is an evolutionary process and needs to involve the relevant stakeholders at each stage. The key stakeholders to be involved in the decision-making are senior managers, HR management, middle / line managers, employees, and employee forums / union representatives. It is necessary for all the stakeholders to have involvement in the consultation and communication process at the critical stages of WLB design / formation, implementation and evaluation

---

Panel 4.1: Management Involvement in Work-Life Balance Policy Design & Choice

The *2007 Work-Life Balance in Ireland* study explored the extent to which HR managers / directors and middle / line managers were involved in WLB policy design and choice.

All HR managers and 82% of middle / line managers report that the middle / line managers/supervisors in their organisations have little or no involvement in the formation of WLB policies but they play a central role in the implementation of these policies.

Research shows that middle / line managers are the channel through which WLB policies and programmes are implemented. Consequently, if middle / line managers have little / no involvement in the formation of WLB policies, they are less likely to endorse and successfully implement these policies and programmes.

Source: McCarthy, Grady & Darcy (2007).

As set out in **Chapter 3**, the level of maturity of WLB policy and practice can vary greatly from one organisation to another, depending on its size, past experience with WLB programmes, employee demand for WLB, etc. Certain WLB programmes may be more suitable for some organisations, depending on the stage of maturity of their WLB policy. **Table 4.2** sets out some of the characteristics of WLB policies and programmes evident at each stage in WLB evolution. Organisations that are new to the WLB agenda (see the formative stage in **Table 4.2**) will tend to focus mostly on their statutory requirements with few discretionary WLB policies and programmes being available to staff. At the other end of the continuum, where organisations have a mature WLB strategy, WLB policy and programmes are effectively linked to the business strategy and many WLB programmes are available to a broad cross-section of staff. In many cases, WLB programme choice is dependent on the level of maturity of WLB strategy and develops gradually over time.

Table 4.2: Work-Life Balance Policies in Operation at Different Stages of Work-Life Balance Evolution

Stage	Characteristics	Evidence
Formative	Compliant with legal requirements. A small number of WLB policies in place.	Policies / procedures in place to meet legal requirements. WLB policies / programmes available to some staff. Queries handled by HR Department. No monitoring of uptake on WLB programmes.
Broadening	Some unconnected WLB policies and procedures in place.	WLB policies available to a wider group but still mainly viewed as designed for specific 'different' groups of employees (for example, working mothers, specific categories or different union memberships). Some managers aware of programme details but most reluctantly accept the necessary evil. Programmes are HR-originated, usually in response to employee / representative demands. Information generally held in HR Department. HR staff monitor the uptake of WLB programmes.
Deepening	Bundle of WLB policies and programmes in place.	Some WLB policies are available to all categories of staff, with many more available to some specific areas. HR initiate introduction of programmes and policies. Policies and programmes seen as response to business needs to attract and retain staff. Most managers are aware of programme aims and details. WLB programmes in the business area are identified and HR skills are developed. Information is actively promoted. HR monitor uptake of WLB programmes and assess why uptake is low.
Mature	Business strategy includes integrated WLB strategy and plans focused on skills, competencies and people-centred outputs of the business.	All WLB policies and practices available to most staff. Organisation responds to identify employee needs. HR monitor uptake of WLB programmes, assess why uptake is low and initiate appropriate action. Motivating, retaining and developing staff seen as critical management competencies and core business needs. Valuing people statements supported by senior managers who are acting as role models. Flexibility to meet business and staff needs is seen as a requisite. Line Managers fully supportive and trained in implementation of policies and programmes and ensure equity and fairness for all employees. HR supporting, instead of driving, WLB.

Source: Work Life Balance Network (2004: 52).

Work-Life Balance Programme Choice & Employee Needs

Employees have differing WLB needs at various stages in their life-cycle. Therefore, employers considering implementation of WLB policies and programmes should consider the personal needs of their employees at various stages of their life to inform their policy choice. This quotation from the *2007 Work-Life Balance in Ireland* study supports this view:

> "Work-life balance is very different for different age groups – they have different needs at different stages of their lives." – Manager, Telecommunications sector.

Table 4.3 presents the various employee life-cycle stages. During an employee's working life, their personal needs are likely to change considerably from stage to stage. The typical age range for each stage is set out, as well as the personal needs of employees during this period. The WLB policies that are most suitable to these needs are presented in the last column. Organisations should consider clearly the age range of employees in their organisation, or in particular business units/divisions where the WLB policy will be introduced. It is imperative that the WLB programmes made available actually suit the needs of the employees. The case studies on Stage 2 (family-oriented), Stage 3 (mid-career) and Stage 4 (pre-retirement) included below demonstrate how employee needs at various life-cycle stages are different and can be accommodated using a variety of approaches.

Table 4.3: Implementation of Work-Life Balance Policies & Programmes to Support Employees' Needs at Various Life-Cycle Stages

Life-cycle	Age	Personal needs	Policy needs
Stage 1: Career-oriented	18-30	Improve qualifications to advance career. Enjoy recreation / hobbies.	Supportive arrangements (gym membership, shop discounts). Education schemes. Flexi-time. On-site medical facilities.
Stage 2: Family-oriented	30-45	Support small children with school and extra curriculum activities. Need / want more personal time. Reduce commuting long distance.	Flexi-time. E-working. Compressed working week – 4 long days, working same hours. 3-day week / 4-day presence in office. Job-sharing. Work-sharing. Part-time. Term-time working / Life-balance time. Supportive arrangements.
Stage 3: Mid-career	45-55	Support children through second and third-level school. Care for elderly parents. Self-care time. Reduce commuting long distances. Up-skilling / personal development / education.	Life-balance time. Reduced working week, 4-day week; 3-day week / 4-day presence in office; 9 days in two weeks. Compressed working week – 4 long days, working same hours. Supportive arrangements.
Stage 4: Pre-retirement	55+	Self-care time. Care for elderly parents.	Life-balance time. Reduced working week, 4-day week; 3-day week / 4-day presence in office; 9 days in two weeks. Compressed working week – 4 long days, working same hours. Supportive arrangements.

Source: Adapted from ABCs of the Kaleidoscope Career Model.[38]

---

[38] Sullivan & Mainiero (2007).

CASE STUDY 4.5

The Electricity Supply Board

Career Life Cycle: Stage 2 - Family or Personal Needs-oriented

Michelle is a senior manager working with the Electricity Supply Board (ESB) in Dublin. Under a WLB arrangement, she works 60% of the normal 36.25 hour working week, over four days. As with full-time workers, she is expected to work additional hours as required by the business. Michelle's reason for opting for reduced working are to take care of her three young children.

Q: Why did you choose to take up the reduced working hours option?
A: It was three years ago, when I was Financial Controller of a business unit, and I spoke to the Finance Director about the possibility of working reduced hours. I suppose we all agreed that the Financial Controller job was not going to work on a reduced hours basis. I stepped out of that role and worked in a project role for two years. That was difficult, because it meant stepping off the management team and it felt a little bit like a demotion - but I had chosen to do it and I knew why I was doing it.

I could have gone down the road of saying that I could hold down my current role but that would have pushed a lot of pressure onto my team members – not only the team working for me, but the management team.

Q: Did availing of WLB initiatives affect your promotional opportunities?
A: No. When a promotional position for senior manager arose, after I had opted for reduced working hours, I applied for it.

It was a real quandary for me. I went through all sorts of questioning before deciding to go for it and spoke to various people [colleagues and senior management] before I put my name in the hat. I find that I strip out unnecessary meetings, lunches, golf outings, etc – however, in doing so, I have to be careful I do not miss out on networking, which is very important. You do struggle to keep that balance.

Q: How has opting for this WLB initiative benefited you?
A: It has meant a huge amount to me, and general happiness in my life

– because I was struggling before that, feeling that I wanted to give more time to my family and my children (and feeling perhaps that they might be suffering a little), and trying to hold down a full-time career. Now I feel my life is more balanced. I did not have to sacrifice either one. If flexible working was not available to me, I could well have been forced to take a career break, resign and opt out of the workforce.

Q: What are the benefits to your organisation?
A: When an organisation loses experienced people who are committed and in whom they have invested over the years, there is a huge amount of knowledge and experience that can be wasted. I was 12 years in the company before I sought to reduce my hours. Organisations can win from offering WLB initiatives, if they are willing to accept that it does not have to be a straight 9am to 5pm five-day week - there can be other ways of working effectively. If organisations have employees who are motivated and happy with a balance in their life, and not feeling stressed, they are going to get more positive employees and productive output.

Q: Is a work-life balance 'role model' important in organisations?
A: Because I avail of reduced working hours, I am more open-minded to facilitating employees in my own team who are seeking greater work-life balance. I believe that the more that managers can see how WLB / flexible working can successfully work, and see that they can be managed in a positive way, then that will give managers the encouragement at least to open their minds towards flexibility for their employees. However, not all job roles are suitable for flexible working, but organisations and employees together need to analyse the role to establish the possibilities for flexibility. I think more can be done by organisations. I meet mothers in the school yard with extraordinary talents and many of them would love to have the opportunity I have to work reduced hours.

– taken from an interview with a senior manager, ESB.

CASE STUDY 4.6

Department of Justice, Equality & Law Reform

Career Life-Cycle: Stage 3 - Mid-career

Martina, a senior manager in the Department of Justice, Equality & Law Reform, avails of a four-day-week work pattern.

She does not avail of this option in order to look after children, which is usually the reason employees use this WLB initiative. Instead, having reached mid-career, she felt that it was time to develop herself further and to take the opportunity to do other things in her life.

She believes that working a four-day working week has many benefits:

"Working a four-day week has been very beneficial, both for me personally and the Department.

I have pursued a qualification in human resources and mediation and this adds value to my role in the Department. Given the nature of the job I do, this would have been extremely difficult to achieve on a five-day week. In addition, working reduced hours gives me the opportunity to devote time to voluntary work with the Special Olympics, which is important to me.

Because I can avail of WLB initiatives, it provides an opportunity to add different dimensions to my life, which is good for me and can have benefits for the employer and others."

– taken from an interview with a Senior Manager, DoJELR.

CASE STUDY 4.7

The Electricity Supply Board (ESB)
Career Life-Cycle: Stage 4 - Pre-Retirement

A male senior manager in the ESB, who is now in stage 4 (pre-retirement) in the career life-cycle, discusses how flexible working as a work-life balance strategy works for him. The WLB flexible working option for this manager is to have every alternative Friday off work. He works nine days out of 10.

Q: Why did you choose to take up the reduced working hours option?
A: At the time I opted to avail of reduced hours, I had 35 years' service in the organisation and always felt that, as people came towards retirement, it was a significant change going from working five days to not working at all. I believe that, if employees have some facility whereby they could work down towards retirement, it would be more beneficial for them.

I found myself in a situation where my children were finishing their education and I didn't have the same demands financially. My partner works a three-day week, and we both play golf on the Friday I am off work, which allows us to have more personal time as we pursue a mutual interest.

Q: Has your workload reduced since opting for reduced hours?
A: I don't think my workload has reduced significantly. I am not conscious of working 10% less than before. It is the same workload and, if part of my work has to be completed before Friday, it will happen. I would stay late one evening if I had to finish something.

Q: Do you think it is more difficult for men to apply for WLB / flexible working?
A: When I was younger, I suppose I had it in the back of my mind that it [availing of WLB initiatives] would impact on my career. Whether that is a balanced perspective or not – I would

have had the belief that the organisation would have perceived it like that. When I did decide to apply for flexible options, I had developed my career as far as I wanted to go and I was happy with my lot.

I think that there is still a view among some people that men on reduced hours are not serious about their career or they are being phased out.

Q: Is a work-life balance 'role model' important in organisations?
A: It has to be driven from the top and has to be part of what the senior people do themselves. If all senior people work 60 hours per week or more, then working long hours becomes the norm and it is hard to believe that WLB is an integral part of the organisation work culture.

Q: How do you see the future of WLB in organisations?
A: It is fitting for organisations to look at new ways of working. Doing nothing is not an option. You are making the organisation a much more attractive place to work if there are WLB programmes in place. If the work environment is comfortable, attractive and can facilitate employees, it benefits the business and the company is more likely to attract and retain people.

When people get to their late 20s and 30s, they are likely to want to work in an environment where they are comfortable. For example, if staff are unhappy when they arrive to work because they have crawled through traffic to be at work at 8.30am and know they cannot leave until 5pm, they are unlikely to be as productive as the staff who have a flexible start and finish time, whereby they can spend less time commuting.

– taken from an interview with a senior manager, ESB.

What Programmes Do Employees Avail of and Why / Why Not?

In an attempt to establish what WLB policies and programmes organisations should make available to employees, it is useful to understand which programmes employees find most useful in terms of managing their work and personal life. The *2007 Work-Life Balance in Ireland* study identifies the WLB programmes and initiatives employees report using. The reasons why employees use these programmes are also presented, as well as the reasons employees do not avail of WLB programmes and practices where they are available in the organisation.

The provision of WLB initiatives by an organisation does not necessarily indicate higher levels of uptake or use by employees. The key factors that affect employee usage of WLB programmes include:

- Increasing awareness of the options and opportunities that are available.

- Greater access to employees at various organisational levels.

- Greater support from management to use WLB programmes.

The most commonly-used WLB / flexible arrangements in the public and private sectors are shown in **Table 4.4** – the percentage of employees who report availing of these arrangements is shown in parentheses.

Table 4.4: The Most Commonly-used Work-Life Balance Arrangements

Public sector	Private sector
<ul><li>Flexi-time (81%).</li><li>Time off in lieu (38%).</li><li>Work-sharing (23%).</li><li>Term-time working (14%).</li><li>Part-time working (14%).</li></ul>	<ul><li>Membership / discounts (53%).</li><li>Time off in lieu (49%).</li><li>Informal flexibility (43%).</li><li>On-site medical facilities (41%).</li><li>Education schemes (40%).</li></ul>

Source: 2007 Work-Life Balance in Ireland *study.*

The use or uptake of temporal WLB arrangements is much higher in the public sector when compared with the private sector, where the most popular programmes used by employees tend to be more supportive in nature rather than focused on reducing working hours and flexible working schedules. However, even in the public sector, the proportion of staff availing of work-sharing, part-time and term-time still can be considered quite low.

Employees' most commonly-cited reasons for availing of WLB programmes are:

- Childcare.

- The desire for more personal time.

- For commuting / traffic reasons.

The *2007 Work-Life Balance in Ireland* study also explored reasons why employees do not avail of various work-life balance programmes where they are available to them. There are interesting differences cited by private sector employees, compared with public sector employees (see **Table 4.5**, which presents these reasons in rank order).

**Table 4.5: Employees' Reasons for Not Engaging in
Work-Life Balance Practices**

	PUBLIC	PRIVATE
1	Already satisfied with my WLB.	Negative career consequences.
2	Negative career consequences.	Not available to me.
3	Not available to me.	Job does not lend itself to flexible practices.
4	Job does not lend itself to flexible practices.	Already satisfied with my WLB.

Source: 2007 Work-Life Balance in Ireland *study.*

Public sector employees cited the fact that they are already satisfied with their work-life balance as the primary reason for not availing of WLB options and arrangements. The second most commonly-cited reason for not availing of WLB programmes in the public sector is the negative impact on career – there is a perception that taking up these policies and practices indicates less career focus and ambition. The third and fourth most often-cited reasons for not engaging in WLB practices for employees in the public sector are that the practices are not available to them in their particular role and that their job does not lend itself to flexible working practices.

Private sector employees cited the impact of negative career consequences of taking up flexible working practices as the top reason for not engaging in flexible working practices and reduced working hours. The second and third most often-cited reasons for not availing of WLB programmes in the private sector are that these programmes are not available to employees or that their job does not lend itself to flexible working. The fourth reason cited for not using WLB programmes is that employees are already satisfied with their work-life balance.

Step 6: A Planned & Systematic Approach for Implementing Work-Life Balance Policies & Programmes

Implementing the WLB policies and programmes deemed most suitable to the organisation and to employees' needs in a planned and systematic manner, as opposed to a 'grace and favour' type approach, is essential. However, striking a balance to meet the business objectives and targets, while also being as flexible as possible for individual employees, is one of the key challenges in implementing work-life balance policies and programmes according to the 2007 *Work-Life Balance in Ireland* study.

These challenges can be addressed in the following ways:

- Managing unrealistic expectations of employees of what the company provides and setting out expectations for employees up-front.

- Developing a strategy that will suit the needs of the organisation, as well as the needs of the employees.

- Making sure that the process is equitable and fair to all employees.

- Ensuring that policies and programmes are clearly formulated and transparent.

- Involving all the stakeholders[39] in the design / formation, implementation and evaluation of the policies and programmes.

---

[39]   See **Chapter 3: Design of WLB Initiatives** - Step 4.

- Changing the way that managers / supervisors manage employees who request, or use, WLB programmes.

When implementing WLB programmes and initiatives, a key issue that impacts the effectiveness of WLB policy operation is determining employee eligibility to use WLB programmes and working arrangements – in other words, which employees can avail of what programmes and whether initiatives are available across the entire organisation and to all staff.

The criteria for eligibility must be set out clearly by the organisation in its work-life balance policy and strategy statements. The criteria used to consider employee eligibility will vary from organisation to organisation depending on business needs, the culture of the organisation, the number employed etc. The criteria used to determine eligibility should be transparent and clearly communicated and hence understood by all employees.

Panel 4.2: Employee Eligibility to Apply for WLB Programmes

In the *2007 Work-Life Balance in Ireland* study, HR managers and middle / line managers report that the majority of employees in their organisations are eligible to avail of WLB policies and programmes.

However, even though employees are eligible to avail of WLB initiatives, 24% and 59% of middle / line managers in the public and private sector respectively report that it is not feasible or practical for all groups of employees to avail of WLB programmes.

The most often-cited reasons why WLB initiatives cannot be made available to all staff in the organisation are that WLB policies and programmes are not compatible with the nature of some jobs, in particular for senior / middle managers' roles, and that they are difficult to operate for certain staff.

Source: 2007 Work-Life Balance in Ireland *study.*

Organisations may wish to consider some of the following key areas when determining employee eligibility to use particular WLB programmes:

- **Operational issues:** Business needs *versus* the employee's needs.
- **Length of service within the organisation:** Typically, most organisations require an employee to have between 26 weeks' and 2 years' service in order to be considered eligible to apply for certain WLB initiatives.
- **Flexibility of timing of the request:** Is it suitable for work patterns and business needs at that time?
- **Whether the employee already is availing of another WLB initiative:** For example, if an employee is availing of job-sharing, he / she may not be able to avail of term-time or life-balance time.
- **Whether the employee has availed of a WLB initiative in the previous 12 months.**

Eligibility issues may be determined at a group level (for example, a business unit / department), whereby particular types of programmes are considered not feasible due to work processes in that area – for example, flexi-time is most unlikely to be a valid WLB option for assembly line operations in a manufacturing environment that uses shift-work.

Once WLB programme eligibility has been decided, a number of steps should be followed in the effective implementation of WLB from receipt of application from the employee to the final decision to allow or reject a request. A planned and systematic process for considering all requests for flexible working should ensure equity and fairness in the implementation of WLB policies and programmes. This process should include the following stages:

1. Request to avail of a WLB initiative.
2. Consideration of the request / arrange meeting with the employee.
3. Grant or refuse the request, including detailed feedback as to how and why the decision was reached.
4. Right of appeal for the employee.

This systematic process should include an indicative timeframe for handling all requests. If applications to avail of WLB initiatives are not dealt with promptly, it can lead to dissatisfaction among employees, resulting in poor employee relations within the organisation. However, the specified time allowed should be reasonable both for the employer and the employee. Employees are also entitled to adequate consideration of their WLB programme request, even where the outcome is not favourable, as the following quotation from a manager who participated in the *2007 Work-Life Balance in Ireland* study highlights:

> "Saying 'No' is the wrong thing to do – if we can facilitate employees, it is important to look at that for employees." – Manager, Medical devices sector.

Table 4.6 presents a planned and systematic procedure for implementing WLB initiatives and programmes. This procedure sets out actions with indicative timeframes that organisations can follow when making decisions on WLB programme implementation from initial receipt of a request from an employee through to the final decision. The various stakeholders who should be involved at each stage is set out, along with forms that can be used by organisations (samples of these forms are shown in **Appendix B**).

Table 4.6: A Planned & Systematic Procedure for Implementing Work-Life Balance Initiatives

	Action	Stakeholders involved	Indicative timeframe	Form to be used *
1	**Application to avail of a WLB initiative** is completed by the employee and forwarded to their middle / line manager.	Employee	Should allow for sufficient time for request to be considered.	**Form 1**
2	**Confirmation of receipt of request** is forwarded to employee.	Middle / line manager	Within 1 week.	**Form 1**
3	**Consideration of request and meeting arranged with employee** to consider request in greater detail.	Middle / line manager; employee; other stakeholders involved in planning	Within 3 weeks of receipt of application.	N/A
4	**Decision to grant or refuse request** is made and employee is formally notified of the decision.	Middle / line manager; other stakeholders affected by the decision; HR Department	Within 6 weeks of receipt of application.	
5a	**Grant request** for WLB initiative and change terms and conditions of employment (if applicable).	Middle / line manager; employee; HR representative	Within 6 weeks of receipt of application.	**Form 2**
5b	**Refuse request** to avail of WLB initiative.	Middle / line manager; employee; HR representative	Within 6 weeks of receipt of application.	**Form 3**
6	**Employee right to appeal** the decision and submits appeal to middle / line manager.	Employee	Within 2 weeks of refusal received.	**Form 4**
7	**Appeal to be considered** and meeting arranged.	Middle / line manager; HR manager; employee; employee representative	Within 2 weeks of receiving the appeal.	N/A
8	**Final decision** on this request made and employee informed.	Middle / line manager; senior HR representative; employee; employee representative	Within 6 weeks of receiving the appeal.	**Form 2** or **Form 3**

* Sample forms are available in **Appendix B**.

Action 1: Request to Avail of a Work-Life Balance Initiative

An application to avail of a WLB initiative should be completed by the employee and submitted to their middle / line manager (see **Form 1** in **Appendix B**). The employee should allow sufficient time for the request to be considered.

Prior to discussing their request with their manager, the employee must consider the issues that may impact upon their application for the WLB initiative:

- How their request to avail of the WLB initiative will impact on their job role.

- Potential challenges in terms of their own work, if their request is granted.

- How their use of the WLB initiative will impact on their colleagues.

The middle / line manager should consider the request for the WLB initiative by taking into account the following:

- Specific circumstances of the business needs / environment. In particular, any decision to accommodate a request for a WLB initiative should consider the core operational needs relating to the business objectives, as well as the employee's needs for flexibility.

- Reasons for making the request – both personal and wider organisational issues.

- Type of change requested – permanent or temporary.

- Proposed implementation date specified.

- The criteria for eligibility.

- The impact that granting the request for the WLB initiative will have on the service / support function and the views of the employee on how this can be dealt with.

- The impact that granting the request for the WLB initiative will have on colleagues in that department / work-group and the employee's views on how this can be dealt with.

- Additional resources needed to continue the workload, to ensure that possible resentment from full-time employees can be eliminated.

Action 2: Confirmation of Receipt of Request to avail of a Work-Life Balance Initiative

The middle / line manager should confirm receipt of a request to avail of a WLB initiative to the employee within one week of receiving the request. Regular communication with employees throughout the process of consideration of their request for a WLB initiative is necessary.

Action 3: Consideration of the Employee Request to avail of a Work-Life Balance Initiative

The middle / line manager considers the employee's request to avail of a WLB initiative and arranges a meeting to discuss in greater detail the request within a specified period of time (for example, within three weeks).

However, prior to this meeting, the middle / line manager should conduct an initial assessment of the request, based on the details contained within the application form. In order to do this, it will be necessary to liaise with the relevant individuals who are involved in the co-ordination and planning of the business needs (targets, customer service), before making any initial decisions on the feasibility of the request.

Consideration of some requests may take longer, where difficulties need to be overcome. Difficulties can range from the negative impact on the business performance at that period of time to inability to re-organise work among existing employees. At the meeting with the employee, the impact of the preferred working arrangement on business performance, together with the impact on existing staff, should be discussed in detail. The views of the employee as to how their request to avail of the WLB initiative will affect the operational service / support function and how it may impact on their work colleagues should be discussed. Furthermore, employees should be expected to consider how these issues might be resolved. These views can be critical to the success or failure of the implementation of the new working arrangement.

If a specific request cannot be accommodated, the manager should seek to work with the individual to try to explore alternatives and agree a compromise that suits both the organisation's business needs and the individual's needs. Managers should consult with the HR Department when this occurs, so that a HR representative can attend the meeting in order to help facilitate a discussion around alternatives and reach a compromise.

Action 4: Decision to Grant the Request to avail of a Work-Life Balance Initiative

The value of a systematic procedure for granting or refusing WLB requests is highlighted in the following quotation from a manager in the *2007 Work-Life Balance in Ireland* study:

> "Having a clear procedure for when decisions are communicated has helped to 'take the emotion out of the process' and ensures that operational considerations are balanced with employees' preferred working arrangements." - Public sector manager, *2007 Work-Life Balance in Ireland* study participant

When all possibilities have been explored by the middle / line manager and a decision is made to accommodate the employee's request to avail of a WLB initiative, the type of change must be clearly defined and a commencement date agreed (see **Form 2** in **Appendix B** for a sample). The change can be:

- **Permanent** – which involves a change not only to the employee's working pattern, but also to their terms and conditions in their contract of employment. When a change is permanent, there will be no automatic right for the employee to revert back to their previous working pattern or their previous job role, if a change of job role was necessary to accommodate their request for the WLB initiative.

- **Temporary** – which involves a change for a specified period of time to enable the needs of the employee at that particular time to be facilitated. Employees accepting a temporary change will revert automaticaliy to their original working pattern at the end of the temporary agreement, but may not revert back to their previous job role, if a change of job role was necessary to accommodate their request for the WLB initiative.

- **Trial** – which involves a change for a short period of time (for example, three months) to test whether the new working arrangement is practical and feasible. A change on a trial basis can apply when the middle / line manager is unsure of the impact that granting the request for the WLB initiative will have on the business needs. This trial period will allow the potential impact of granting the WLB initiative to be assessed, thus allowing a more informed decision to be made on the request. Employees accepting a trial basis change will revert automatically to their original working pattern at the end of the agreement, unless a new agreement is reached.

Action 5a: Agreement to Grant the Request to Avail of a Work-Life Balance Initiative

When a request for a WLB initiative has been agreed, the employee must be notified in writing. The changes pertaining to this WLB initiative must be clearly outlined. The following factors need to be considered.

(1)   **Contract of employment**: If a change is permanent, this will require a change in the terms and conditions of the employee's contract of employment. These changes must be clearly documented in writing. *If the change appropriate to the WLB initiative agreed involves reducing the employee's working hours, and / or they avail of time off without pay, the following issues need to be considered in their contract of employment:*

    (a)   **Remuneration**: salary and allowances will also be reduced on a *pro rata* basis.

    (b)   **Annual leave entitlement / public holidays**: The standard rules for these entitlements will apply (refer to Organisation of Working Time Act 1997).

    (c)   **Pension / superannuation**: The period of unpaid leave does not count for superannuation purposes. An individual may opt to pay both their own and the company contributions for the period of unpaid leave or reduced working time, at the company's discretion.

(2)   **Date of return to original working pattern at the end of the agreement**: If an employee is granted a temporary or trial period change, a date of return to their original working pattern, if the new pattern is deemed unsuitable, must be agreed and confirmed in writing to the employee.

(3)   **Extension of time (optional)**: An agreement with an employee to avail of a WLB initiative should include an option to extend the trial / temporary period. If an extension of the time to change the working pattern is agreed between the middle / line manager and the employee, it should be documented in writing. A copy of the new agreement should be provided to the individual and the HR Department for documentation.

(4)   **Monitoring and review process**: A monitoring and review process should apply to all WLB initiatives – for example, after the initial three months in operation and at six-monthly intervals thereafter.

(5)   **Job role**: If changes pertaining to the WLB initiative being granted involves the employee moving to a new job role, the position with regard to returning to their original job role needs to be considered and clearly documented at the outset.

    (a)   If availing of the WLB initiative involves a *permanent* change to the employee's contract of employment, but necessitated the employee to move to a new job role to be accommodated, the employee will have no automatic right to return to their original job role, if their needs change.

    (b)   If availing of a WLB initiative involves a *temporary* change to the employee's contract of employment, but necessitated the employee to move to a new job role to be accommodated, they will have no automatic right to return to their original job role, but this can be changed at the employer's discretion.

    (c)   If availing of a WLB initiative involves a change on a *trial basis* to the employee's contract of employment, but necessitates the employee to move to a new job role to be accommodated, they should be given the option to return to their original job role at the end of the temporary / trial period agreement if desired.

Action 5b: Decision to Refuse an Employee's Request to Avail of a Work-Life Balance Initiative

> "The challenge is to say 'No' to some employees. However, you cannot say 'Yes' to all employees at the same time, but managers must have an open mind to saying 'Yes' and work towards flexibility." - Middle manager, Professional services sector, participant in the *2007 Work-Life Balance in Ireland* study.

It may not be possible to fulfil all employee requests to avail of particular WLB initiatives, at the same time, despite such policies and programmes being in place. If a request from an employee to avail of a WLB initiative cannot be accommodated at a particular time, following full and careful consideration, together with all the alternatives having been explored, the middle / line manager must inform the employee in writing of that decision using **Form 3** (see **Appendix B**). The rationale for refusing the employee's application to avail of a WLB initiative must be clearly stated.

Possible reasons for refusal of requests for flexible working may include:

- The damaging impact on the performance of the organisation; the ability to meet customer requirements; or the quality of work and service to customers.
- Inability to re-organise work among existing employees.
- Inability to recruit additional staff to cover the change in working pattern.
- The burden of additional costs.

An employee should be given the right to appeal any decision where they are not fully satisfied and the procedure should accommodate this.

Action 6: Employee Right to Appeal a Decision for Refusal to Avail of a Work-Life Balance Initiative

If an employee appeals against the employer's decision not to grant their application to avail of a WLB initiative, they should set out the grounds for appeal in writing using **Form 4** (see **Appendix 4**) within a specified period of time (for example, 14 days). This form should be forwarded to their middle / line manager who originally made the decision to refuse the request.

Action 7: Consideration of the Appeal

The middle / line manager should inform their senior manager and a senior HR representative of the request for an appeal and should forward all the relevant paperwork for consideration. The appeal should then be considered by all the stakeholders involved (senior and middle / line management, HR management and the employee), taking into account all the previous investigations and the rationale for refusal of the request for the WLB initiative.

Following a full and careful analysis of the appeal, a meeting should be arranged with the employee within a specified period of time (for example, 2 weeks) to discuss the appeal. The employer can be represented by the middle / line manager, and / or senior manager and a HR representative. The employee can opt to be accompanied by a staff colleague, an employee forum representative or a union representative.

Action 8: Final Decision

Following the meeting, the employer should endeavour to make a decision on the appeal within a reasonable period of time (for example, 14 days) and the employee should be informed in writing of the outcome.

If the final decision is to accept the request to avail of a WLB initiative, the request should be processed using **Form 2** (see **Appendix B**). On the other hand, if the final decision is made to reject the appeal, this decision should be processed on **Form 3** (see **Appendix B**).

The decision made on appeal is final. A copy of the decision should be forwarded to the stakeholders involved. Documentation on the final decision should be sent to the HR department so that details can be recorded on the WLB initiatives requests register on the HR database.[40] This register can be a useful tool to monitor and evaluate WLB initiatives and the outcomes. All relevant documentation should be filed on the employee's personnel file in the HR department.

The sixth step in the model proposed in this book, as set out above, details the issues to be considered when implementing work-life balance at the employee level. The role of the middle / line manager is critical at all stages in this process. Step 7 of the model explores what training should be delivered to ensure managers, and various other stakeholders, have the knowledge, skill and ability to effectively implement and manage WLB policy and practice.

Step 7: Training Programmes for Implementation

It is important for managers to have the 'skill', as well as the 'will', to manage WLB effectively. A customised training programme is useful to ensure that the operation of WLB initiatives is clearly understood by all the stakeholders, including senior managers and middle / line managers.

Panel 4.3: Work-Life Balance Training

The *2007 Work-Life Balance in Ireland* study reports that only a small percentage of organisations use training initiatives aimed at implementation of WLB policies and programmes. The study findings reveal that organisations that introduce WLB programmes will have a policy in place but that the policy is usually implemented in an *ad hoc* way.

The most common method of training managers on WLB was providing a policy to them via the intranet, and on some occasions, discussing this policy at a management meeting.

Source: 2007 Work-Life Balance in Ireland *study.*

---

[40]   See **Chapter 5, Monitoring & Evaluating WLB Initiatives**, for a sample.

According to a CIPD study,[41] organisations use many methods to overcome the challenges of implementation of WLB initiatives. Training is critical to change the mindset to ensure that managers have the 'will' initially and then the 'skill' for implementation.

Suggested training methods to ensure more effective implementation of WLB policies and programmes include:

- **Educating managers** to enable them to consider the business case for flexible working via training sessions.

- **Involvement of managers in workshops** to formulate and develop policies and programmes and, in so doing, gaining buy-in from them to implement the programmes successfully. In addition, training can support changing the mindset of managers on how employees can work in different way – for example, changing from a face-time to a results-oriented culture.

- **Coaching managers** to be more open-minded when dealing with WLB initiative requests about alternative ways of working.

- **Creating case studies** to showcase examples of different employees taking up flexible working arrangements and the benefits to the business, as well as the individual.

- **Involvement of senior management** in promoting flexible working to demonstrate their active support for the programmes.

In recent CIPD research,[42] it was reported that the managers did not believe that implementation of WLB initiatives required an entirely new skillset, rather they believed it was a generic competence of management. Therefore, implementation of WLB initiatives underlines the need for managers to be competent and confident in their ability to manage the performance of their team.

Nonetheless, there is a need to change the mindset of some managers in terms of managing staff working non-traditional patterns. For example, managing employees who are e-working means that managers cannot 'see' the work application and output of the team on a daily basis and thus may require different management processes. Measuring the performance of employees against their objectives still remains an important indicator that employees are performing. However, empowering employees to achieve, regardless of where the employee works, is essential to having an open mind to WLB initiatives (see **Case Study 4.8 – Dell** on using training as a tool to create a strong work-life culture).

---

[41] CIPD (2006b).
[42] CIPD (2006b).

CASE STUDY 4.8

Dell Ireland

Using Training as a Tool to Create a Strong Work-Life Culture

Dell is a leading global systems and services company in the ICT sector and has over 4,500 people employed between its Limerick EMEA manufacturing facility and Cherrywood, Dublin. Ingrid Devin, EMEA Diversity & Inclusion Manager, talks about using training as a tool to create a strong work-life culture.

Q: Why is work-life balance important for Dell?

A: Results from our internal surveys have shown that implementing work-life balance initiatives is a key attraction and retention tool. There is a new work culture emerging now, where employees are searching for a better work-life balance. Employees are seeking more flexibility in the way they work and, if the business can support it, we will do our best to make it happen.

Q: What was involved in the project?

A: To create a strong work-life culture, it is essential that managers understand the importance of work-life balance and can implement and support our work-life policies and initiatives.

To achieve this, we developed two training modules on work-life effectiveness:

- **Lessons in Leadership on Work-Life Effectiveness:** Workshops are delivered by our senior executive management team and cascaded down throughout the organisation. The objectives of the training are to clarify Dell's approach to work-life effectiveness, to raise any organisational myths / incorrect assumptions that are inhibiting people from taking ownership of the work-life effectiveness programmes and to drive consistency in our approach to work-life across teams within Dell. The

training has resulted in many lively discussions about how we can ensure our employees in Dell can gain balance in their work and non-work lives.

- **Management Training:** This training is designed to build awareness among managers of all the policies and initiatives available in the organisation. It also deals with how the initiatives can be implemented effectively and the challenges that may follow. Many of the challenges can be overcome by careful planning. It is necessary to tease out the individual needs and priorities of the team in relation to work-life, and remember that one size does not fit all. The key thing to remember is that you need to be open to flexible options, bearing in mind the business needs.

Q: How do you know whether the training has been successful?

A: Internal surveys have shown an increase in work-life scores. In addition, Dell Ireland has been recognised with a Diversity Award by the prestigious Chamber of Commerce Awards for Corporate Social Responsibility, with a special mention for the work the company has achieved in flexible working and gender over the past year.

Q: What are the greatest challenges around work-life balance?

A: The challenge is to change the mindset of both employees and managers about the importance of work-life balance. However, to be a truly diverse company, there has to be a strong focus on work-life and the different requirements of our diverse workforce.

- taken from an interview with Ingrid Devin, EMEA Diversity & Inclusion Manager, Dell.

Chapter Summary

A wide variety of work-life balance initiatives are available to organisations and there are advantages and disadvantages associated with each. Choosing the WLB initiatives that best suit an organisation is dependent on what stage of the WLB evolutionary process the organisation is at. All the relevant stakeholders should be involved in the consultation and communication process at the critical stages of design / formation, implementation and evaluation of the initiatives.

Furthermore, employees have differing needs at various stages in their life-cycle and many workers are now defining career success in different ways. Employers considering designing and implementing WLB policies and programmes need to take cognisance of employee personal needs at the various life-cycle stages to inform their policy needs.

WLB policies and programmes should be implemented in a planned and systematic way, as opposed to a 'grace and favour' manner. In addition, striking a balance to ensure the organisation meets its objectives, as well as considering the employee needs, is critical.

The various stages of how an employee can apply to avail of a WLB initiative, including the selection criteria and timeframes, should be set out in a clear and transparent manner as part of WLB policy.

Finally, training for managers is a critical element to implementing WLB initiatives to ensure they have both the 'skill' and the 'will' for successful WLB policy and programme implementation.

5: Monitoring & Evaluating WLB Policies & Programmes

"Unfortunately, [work-life balance] programmes are frequently glitter without substance or accolades without application."
*– **Perry M. Christensen**[43]*

Perry Christensen's rather gloomy view of WLB programmes above draws attention to some of the key criticisms of the work-life balance field to-date: that tangible evidence as to their benefits and effects is not well-known, since many firms fail to monitor and evaluate their WLB programmes and initiatives adequately. There have been many advances in terms of work-life balance policy at an organisational and socio-political level, but there tends to be less focus on the actual practice and implementation. A significant gap remains in the work-life balance landscape, where organisations do not engage in monitoring and evaluating how work-life balance policies and programmes operate in practice, the impact such programmes have on employees and the business, and the overall effectiveness of the work-life balance strategy and practice within their organisation. In today's environment, systematic evaluation of how well work-life balance initiatives operate is essential to the survival of these initiatives.[44]

*This chapter sets out the challenges involved in evaluating WLB initiatives and provides guidance on how to demonstrate the 'value' of WLB to senior decision-makers in the organisation. Consequently, it deals with step 8 (see **Figure 5.1**) of the best practice implementation model as set out in **Chapter 1**. The chapter emphasises the importance of monitoring and evaluating WLB policies and programmes and provides a five-stage systematic approach that organisations can use to measure and quantify the various components, thus providing them with the business-critical information they require.*

---

[43]   Christensen (1999).
[44]   Fried (1999).

The Challenge of Evaluation

Research on the state of many HR functions today concludes that "senior managers look at all the fragments and are not clear how the HR function as a whole adds value".[45] A key challenge for HR professionals is to demonstrate the value of WLB initiatives and, in order to do so, a process must be in place to monitor and evaluate such programmes. In addition, organisations need to align WLB policies and programmes with other HR activities, such as compensation and benefits and performance management, in order to maximise the true potential of such programmes and initiatives. Research conducted on behalf of CIPD[46] found that some organisations consider WLB policies and programmes as a separate element, with no alignment to the overall HR function or its constituent parts. If WLB policies and programmes are to be embraced fully and valued by the organisation, they must form an integrated part of the HR management function, with real value-adding potential to the overall company bottom line and hence profitability.

Monitoring and evaluating WLB policies and programmes is a somewhat new process. In the past, evaluation has been unsystematic and based primarily on anecdotal evidence.[47] HR professionals have recognised the need to evaluate the effectiveness of company HR interventions but there seems to be real challenges in ensuring practitioners have the skills and tools to achieve this. Research[48] found that some of the challenges reported for the lack of evaluation of HR policies and practices are that:

- Practitioners find 'serious' evaluation to be too time-consuming and report that there is no easy system they can use.

- Practitioners find that line managers rarely show interest in 'traditional' evaluation data.

- Only a small percentage of organisations in the UK relate the effect of HR interventions to the bottom line.

However, many forward-thinking HR practitioners strongly advocate spending more time and effort on follow-up activities to ensure that the WLB policies and programmes themselves are effective, that they are aligned to the strategic objectives to meet the business needs of the organisation, that they are cost-effective and, finally, that the initiatives available meet the needs of employees to enable them to achieve a greater work-life balance.

The evidence suggests that WLB initiatives are considered to have very real value-adding potential and that there is considerable frustration at the lack of perceived acceptance of this by senior and middle / line management, due to a lack of 'traditional' financial data linking WLB to the bottom line. The following quotation is typical of this view and suggests that WLB initiatives deliver more value to organisations than HR professionals are able to demonstrate, due to the lack of evaluation:

> "The perception of some managers is that they are short-changed – they feel they don't get as much out of employees on WLB options – for example, a 50% worker does not have the same commitment as a full-time employee. However, my experience is that such an employee can give more. I have no statistical evidence but my experience to-date, and I have quite a lot of experience as a manager, is that

---

45   Gratton (2003).
46   CIPD (2005).
47   Edwards *et al.* (2003).
48   CIPD (2006c) and CIPD (2007c).

employees who avail of WLB options can and do deliver." – *Manager, Public sector, 2007 Work-Life Balance in Ireland study*

Therefore, the need for the systematic collection and analysis of data on WLB initiatives to prove their 'value', both to the organisation and the employee, is essential. The available anecdotal evidence as to the effectiveness of WLB programmes sometimes can be dismissed in the absence of hard data that demonstrates a real effect in monetary terms. If lessons are to be learned and WLB programmes improved, then organisations need to adopt a systematic approach to monitoring and evaluating what is working and what is not, from a programmatic, organisational and individual perspective. All initiatives need to be evaluated continually and changes made where necessary, in a continuous and emerging process. As the business needs change and the strategy of the organisation changes, so too will it be necessary to review the various HR strategies that support this. WLB initiatives are no different in this respect than compensation and benefits, performance management and training and development. Findings from the *2007 Work-Life Balance in Ireland* study show that little or no monitoring and evaluation of WLB initiatives currently is taking place in Irish organisations (see **Panel 5.1**). This lack of evaluation needs to be addressed and so this chapter describes how organisations can monitor and evaluate WLB initiatives.

Panel 5.1: Measuring the Effects of Work-Life Balance Policies & Programmes

HR managers / directors and middle / line managers who participated in the *2007 Work-Life Balance in Ireland* study were asked how they measured the effectiveness of WLB policies and programmes in their organisations.

The study found that, in practice, organisations do not measure these effects in any formal or systematic way. The evidence reported about positive and negative WLB effects is anecdotal. When managers were asked how they knew about the effects of WLB, some of the replies included reference to "my gut feeling from interaction with employees", "personal experience" and "my perception".

In some of the organisations surveyed, the effectiveness of WLB was deduced from employee attitude surveys, performance management conversations, and one-to-one discussions with employees. However, none of these methods directly monitored or evaluated WLB programme effectiveness.

There is a need to have tangible measurements in relation to the effects of implementing WLB policies and programmes so that the real 'value' to the organisation can be depicted if work-life balance strategy is to be effectively achieved.

Source: 2007 Work-Life Balance in Ireland *study.*

The Challenge to Show 'Value'

Senior decision-makers are becoming more aware that investment in their employees is essential if they are to achieve their business objectives through their people. For organisations to manage their HR investment effectively, they require information that is relevant and up-to-date, to enable them to assess the extent to which that investment is contributing to organisational performance.

Research from CIPD[49] highlights the importance of delivering and validating cost-effective and collaborative HR processes that are aligned with the organisation's strategic priorities. In addition, CIPD emphasises the importance of ensuring that the processes deliver value to the organisation and that resources are deployed in a cost-effective way. Consequently, there is a continuous and urgent need for HR professionals to be able to demonstrate how work-life balance programmes add value to their organisation, if senior decision-makers are to maintain their commitment to invest in these programmes.

Evaluation programmes continue to be plentiful, systems are constantly recommended, and still little is done by organisations in measuring the value of HR processes such as WLB initiatives. While concepts like return on investment (ROI) have become popular for establishing the costs and benefits associated with various HR investments, many organisations still pay little attention to the purpose of evaluating HR policies and programmes.[50] Research in the UK found that only 25% of organisations formally monitor the take-up of flexible working and only 20% evaluated the effectiveness of one or more of their flexible working practices in the previous year.[51]

Research[52] indicates that a 'one-size-fits-all' set of metrics to establish the value of HR processes such as work-life balance is inappropriate – a tailored and customised approach is required:

- It is necessary to align the evaluation procedure and investment to the organisational strategic priorities – for example, how does the WLB initiative(s) support organisational goal(s)? How can this be proven? How can this be measured? How is effectiveness established? How does this initiative(s) fit with other HR and organisational initiatives – is there alignment?

- A variety of methods should be used to assess and evaluate the contribution of WLB initiatives, drawing on both qualitative and quantitative data. Data can be sourced from the HR database, employee satisfaction / climate surveys, exit interviews, employee-manager face-to-face meetings, relevant forums / focus groups, and performance appraisal meetings.

- Establishing the most appropriate methods of reporting the findings on the value of work-life balance policies and programmes is essential.

The set of metrics used and the level of investment to demonstrate the 'value' of WLB investment often will be determined by what stage the organisation is at in the WLB evolution. **Table 5.1** sets out the WLB monitoring and evaluation practices that typify each stage in the evolution of WLB.

---

49 CIPD (2007b).
50 CIPD (2005).
51 CIPD (2005).
52 CIPD (2007d).

Table 5.1: Monitoring & Evaluating Work-Life Balance Policies & Programmes at Different Stages of Work-Life Balance Evolution

Stage	Characteristics	Evidence
Formative	Assessment based on inputs rather than outputs. Cost-focused. HR monitoring involves absenteeism, headcount numbers, hours worked. Disciplinary processes are corrective-orientated. Recruitment and retention problems viewed as environment-imposed.	No formal staff surveys in place or WLB not formally assessed in staff surveys. Anecdotal evidence on why employees are leaving the organisation – usually linked to poor person-organisation fit or dissatisfaction with salary. Perceived underperformance is complained about, not objectively assessed and no improvement plans developed.
Broadening	Assessment based on work outputs but does not include WLB indicators. Cost-focused. HR monitoring now involves some 'people' analysis (e.g. staff exit interviews). Initial re-active policies in place.	Limited WLB staff surveys in place. Formal performance management processes in place but do not include HR indicators. WLB policies costed but not valued. Recruiting and retaining staff seen as a HR problem, not a management performance indicator.
Deepening	Assessment is based on work output requirements and includes WLB indicators. Value / cost-benefit analysis carried out on some staff policies and programmes. HR monitoring linked to business needs.	Pro-active staff surveys in place. Costing of recruitment and re-training is included in business area costs and in management performance indicators. Formal performance management processes are in place and include measures to ensure that a long hours culture does not exist or develop.
Mature	Staff viewed as value-adding, not as a cost. Assessment based on clear business goals. Value / cost-benefit analysis carried out on some staff policies and programmes. Continuous pro-active planning towards attracting, developing and retaining quality staff is a core business measure.	Pro-active staff surveys in place. Results analysed, trends identified and solutions developed jointly by business areas and HR. Formal performance management in place, measurement includes HR indicators at all levels. WLB policies and initiatives reviewed and monitored in a systematic manner.

Source: Work Life Balance Network (2004: 54).

When the WLB strategy has evolved to the desired or appropriate level in the organisation, a systematic approach to monitoring and evaluating the WLB initiatives should be adopted. However, organisations should continue to review and extend the evaluation process as they develop their WLB policies and programmes in line with the organisation's strategic priorities and goals.

In the next section, a five-stage approach for systematic monitoring and evaluation of WLB initiatives, as set out in **Figure 5.1**, is presented.

Step 8: A Systematic Approach to Monitoring & Evaluating Work-Life Balance Initiatives

The five stages necessary for successful monitoring and evaluating WLB programmes are:

1. Identifying the purpose of the evaluation.
2. Determining the methods for gathering data.
3. Gathering and analysing the data.
4. Linking the data gathered to the bottom line.
5. Making recommendations, based on the findings of the evaluation.

Figure 5.1: A Five-Stage Systematic Approach to Monitoring & Evaluating Work-Life Balance Initiatives

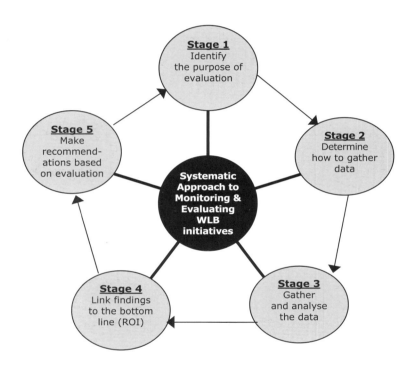

Stage 1: Identify the Purpose of the Evaluation

The purpose of any evaluation should be determined from the outset and the objectives for the evaluation process should be identified at three levels: programmatic, organisational and individual:[53]

Level 1: Programmatic

The purpose of the evaluation at this level is to examine the programmes themselves. Issues to consider can include:

---

[53] Edwards *et al.* (2003).

- **Offering WLB initiatives that will enable the organisation to retain a competitive advantage:** Does the organisation want to be the leader, one of the leaders or average in the WLB arena? Do the WLB programmes match the position it has adopted? These decisions must be aligned to the business strategy and a cost-benefit analysis approach should be used to determine their value.

- **Promoting and increasing awareness of work-life balance:** Is the organisation actively promoting WLB among its employees? Are employees fully aware of the initiatives available to them?

- **Encouraging usage of the initiatives:** What is the level of take-up among the employees at whom the WLB initiatives are targeted? How many requests for WLB initiatives have been submitted, how many accepted, refused or postponed? What were the reasons for refusal or postponement? Are the initiatives implemented in a fair and equitable manner?

Level 2: Organisational

The purpose of the evaluation at an organisational level is to examine the link between the WLB programmes and organisational outcomes. To assess this link, the following are some of the issues that should be explored:

- **Good employee relations:** How positive or negative are employee relations in the organisation? Can these results be directly linked to the availability of WLB initiatives?

- **Increased productivity:** Has there been consistency in meeting production targets, irrespective of WLB programme implementation?

- **Reduced absenteeism:** Is there a decrease in absenteeism, as a result of implementing certain WLB initiatives?

- **Increased retention of valued employees:** Is the organisation losing employees with specialised skills because of inflexibility on WLB issues?

- **Improved recruitment:** Is the organisation seen as an 'employer of choice', which enables it to attract the skills it requires from a wider audience? Does the WLB policy and practice help in creating the 'employer of choice' brand?

- **Promoting a results-based culture:** Has the organisation a supportive culture towards WLB? Do employees feel empowered to work off-site (for example, e-working)? Do employees feel that availing of WLB initiatives could have negative career consequences?

Level 3: Individual

The objective of evaluation at an individual level is to assess the link between WLB initiatives and individual outcomes. To measure individual outcomes, the following factors should be considered:

- **Self-fulfilment:** How fulfilled are employees on and off the job (in their work and personal / family lives)? Do they intend to stay with the organisation? What is their level of job satisfaction?

- **Manageable workload:** How manageable is the employees' workload? Do employees feel that the workload they are expected to complete is reasonable? Is it necessary to work long hours to manage their workload? Do employees availing of reduced working hours feel they are expected to complete the same workload as they did when they were working full-time hours?

- **Balance of work and personal / family life:** Are employees satisfied with their own work-life balance? Does work interfere too much with their personal / non-work life or does the personal / non-work life interfere with the work domain?

- **Positive effects for employees:** Do employees experience a positive spill-over from work to their personal / non-work domain and *vice-versa*?[54]

In summary, the purpose of implementing WLB initiatives is to influence positively both organisational and individual outcomes. Therefore, identifying when the objectives are reached – and when they are not – is central to monitoring and evaluating WLB initiatives. In other words, evaluation is an intervention to check alignment and to reinforce the 'value' of such programmes to the organisation.[55]

When the purpose of the evaluation is established, the methods for gathering the data, the questions to ask, metrics to use and what stakeholders should be involved, needs to be determined. In this context, evaluation is about ensuring there is relevant, integrated and continuous understanding with regard to the effectiveness of the initiatives.

Stage 2: Determine Methods for Gathering Data – 'How' to Evaluate

The 'how' includes gathering data from the major stakeholder groups: the HR function, senior managers, middle / line managers, and individual employees.

The tools used for evaluation are a set of analytical instruments that can be both quantitative and qualitative. The quantitative instruments will collect data that can be linked to the programme and organisational objectives and the business outcomes. The qualitative instruments evaluate the perceptions of employees, which can be linked to the programmatic, organisational and individual outcomes. In addition, the real contribution of the WLB initiatives on various outcomes cannot be assessed in isolation from various other potential influences – in other words, is the WLB policy the only factor that is causing the positive outcomes? Could other factors such as job satisfaction, motivation, commitment and employee-fulfilment actually be having a positive effect on organisational outcomes, such as lower turnover, reduced absenteeism and increased productivity?

The methods to gather quantitative data include:

- **HR database:** Quantitative data for evaluating WLB initiatives can be obtained from the HR database. A WLB initiative request register (see **Table 5.2**), which should be recorded on a database, typically contains information such as number of employees participating in WLB initiatives and the breakdown of type of initiative being availed of (for example, job sharing, flexi-time, career break or education). In addition, a demographic profile of the age, gender, employment category, and level / position in the organisation should be available. Finally, information on the number of requests from employees to avail of the different WLB initiatives, the reasons for these requests, the number accepted / refused or postponed, the reasons for refusal or postponement, and the number of appeals should be recorded. This information can identify potential problem areas within the business units where WLB initiatives are posing challenges for management or where requests do not appear to be given sufficient consideration.

- **Questionnaires or employee satisfaction / climate surveys:** These can be a useful method to gather quantitative WLB data. An electronic or paper version of these questionnaires can be distributed by the HR function, either specifically-oriented

[54] Greenhaus & Powell (2006).
[55] CIPD (2007b).

towards WLB policies and programmes or included as a significant section in an overall employee satisfaction / climate survey. However, this method of gathering data can have a low return rate and the questionnaire needs to be very carefully designed and piloted (to check for, amongst other things, question purpose and clarity, understanding, and time taken for completion). However, surveys are useful in large organisations, where interviews and focus groups may be too time-consuming. Additionally, asking the same questions via a staff survey at regular intervals provides an opportunity for HR practitioners to monitor changing perceptions in relation to WLB initiatives over a period of time. Questionnaires that receive the backing of senior managers generally have much higher response rates (for example, where senior managers ask their direct reports to complete the questionnaire / survey).

Table 5.2: Work-Life Balance Initiative Request Register

Category	Age	Gender	Employ-ment Category	Level 1-5	No. Requests	Reason for request	No. Accepted	No. refused	No. appealed	Reason for refusal
Job-sharing										
Reduced hours										
Part-time										
Flexi-time										
Term-time / Life-balance time										
Career break										
Education scheme										
Other										

Employment Category	Level in the organisation
A Support	1 Direct (e.g. operative)
B Professional	2 Indirect (e.g. clerical, semi-skilled)
C Managerial	3 Professional (e.g. technician, engineer, accountant)
	4 Middle / line manager / supervisor
	5 Senior manager

Source: Adapted from Ernst & Young *case study, CIPD (2006b).*

The methods for gathering qualitative data include:

- **Questionnaire / employee satisfaction surveys** can be used by generating information using open-ended questions in the survey. This can allow employees to include comments and suggestions, which can be a valuable source of data.

- **Focus groups** can allow for discussion and in-depth exploration on how effective existing WLB policies and programmes are and what level of awareness employees have of these initiatives. Focus group membership can be determined by department / business unit / section, if specific feedback and employee input is required. However, focus groups take time and are usually limited to a small number of employees being involved to be effective.

- **Feedback from performance appraisals** can yield useful information on WLB effectiveness. Employee satisfaction with their own WLB and working patterns can be discussed at a performance appraisal meeting. This feedback can be channelled back to the HR function to enhance evaluation of the WLB programmes and to determine how aligned the WLB initiatives are to employee needs. However, research found that performance appraisal interviews are a much under-used source of gathering data on the value of WLB policies and programmes.[56] If used effectively, they can give the organisation an opportunity to link the findings of this process to the organisational strategy, plans and metrics.

- **Feedback from employees** is a particularly useful method for gathering data on how satisfied employees are with their work-life balance. It encourages employees to think about the WLB policies and programmes that exist and how they can gain access to them if they have a need to do so. Additionally, when employees are considering availing of a WLB programme, it gives them an opportunity to discuss the impact (if any) the programme may have on their job role / workload and their colleagues and allows them to put forward solutions to be considered, which can help to reduce negative impact. This involvement supports ownership of, and responsibility for, the successful implementation of the programme they wish to avail of. Organisations can also take the opportunity to seek feedback from middle / line managers about the impact of WLB policies and programmes for their staff – for example, different behaviours and attitudes demonstrated by employees while on or returning from availing of WLB programmes.

Stage 3: Gather & Analyse the Data – 'What' to Evaluate?

'What' to measure is determined by the objectives of the evaluation and whether the focus is at a programmatic, organisational and / or individual level (as set out in Stage 1 above). The purpose of evaluating at the different levels is to provide feedback on the elements of the work-life balance programmes that need to be improved, sustained, reduced or removed. Evaluation can also provide valuable information on the effectiveness of any new programmes or initiatives that have been implemented.

The measures set out in **Table 5.3** can be described as relatively 'hard' metrics and 'soft' measures. Both sets of measures can be valuable in retaining the support of senior management and can assist in winning the support of middle / line managers for successful implementation, together with providing valuable feedback on the effectiveness of the initiatives. In addition, arguably the most difficult part of the process is linking the outcomes to the bottom line to show return on investment.

---

[56] McCarthy *et al.* (2008).

Table 5.3: What Should Be Measured / Evaluated?

Hard metrics – relating the implementation of WLB initiatives to:	Soft measures – relating the implementation of WLB initiatives to:
Level 1: Programmatic Outcomes	
Business strategy, objectives and competitive advantage. Up-take / usage of various WLB initiatives by employees.	Promotion of work-life balance. Increasing awareness among employees and management of the different programmes on offer.
Level 2 : Organisational Outcomes	
Business outputs Increased productivity. Reduced absenteeism. Increased retention. Improved recruitment.	Good employee relations. Promoting a results-based culture.
Level 3: Individual Outcomes	
	Managing the workload. Self-fulfilment for employee on and off the job. Balancing work and personal / family life. Enhanced employee well-being. Motivation and commitment.

Source: Adapted from CIPD (2005) and Edwards et al. (2003).

Level 1: Measuring & Evaluating at the Programmatic Level

Do the various WLB initiatives assist the organisation in achieving its strategy and competitive advantage?

A valuable exercise to obtain relevant data with regard to competitive advantage is to benchmark WLB policies and programmes against those of other similar organisations. Different WLB programmes may have differing effects on competitive advantage and, therefore, it is important to identify which programmes deliver best results. This can be achieved by comparing the organisation against its competitors or other suitable comparator organisations. Such benchmarking should identify examples of good practice, as well as identify gaps and shortcomings in WLB offerings. The sector (public or private) and size of the organisation will influence the type of initiatives available. The organisation then can determine how appropriate its WLB policies and practices are in comparison to other organisations, as well as understanding how WLB contributes to the achievement of business objectives and competitive advantage. From this assessment, the organisation can determine what position on the WLB continuum is most suitable – from not focusing on work-life balance on one end, to designing and operating sophisticated WLB practices at the other end of the scale.[57]

Are work-life balance initiatives promoted in the organisation? Have managers and employees a good awareness of WLB policies and options?

There is sometimes a gap between HR policies and HR practices, whereby certain HR initiatives are well-documented on paper in the organisation but, in practice, the initiatives

---

[57]   Edwards *et al.* (2003).

are not well-embedded in the organisation. Work-life balance initiatives are no different – if WLB policies and initiatives are not well-understood by managers and employees, then their usage and uptake will be limited. It is important, therefore, to ensure that supervisors / line managers are aware of the various WLB policies and practices to enable them to promote these practices to employees.

The level of awareness that supervisors / line managers and employees have of the existing WLB initiatives can be captured using focus groups. Useful questions to generate discussion in a focus group can be:

- Are you aware of the WLB initiatives offered by this organisation?

- Have you availed of any WLB initiatives, if so which one(s)?

Furthermore, quantitative data on promoting WLB initiatives can be collected using a questionnaire / employee satisfaction / climate survey. This can be addressed by including statements in the questionnaire, where employees are asked to indicate on a 5-point scale whether they agree or disagree with various statements assessing WLB knowledge and awareness (5 = strongly agree and 1 = strongly disagree). Statements may include:

- It is easy to find out about work-life balance initiatives within my organisation.

- Managers / supervisors in this organisation are sympathetic towards employees' personal / non-work commitments.

What is the take-up / use of WLB initiatives among various groups?

The HR database and WLB initiative request register (see **Table 5.2**) can provide data on take-up rates for the different WLB programmes on offer – for example, percentages of staff using different programmes, demographic details, job category and level in the organisation. Additionally, further evaluation can be carried out using a questionnaire to determine awareness and take-up, by listing the WLB initiatives available in the organisation and asking questions such as:

- Job-sharing: Is this initiative available in your organisation? *and*

- Do you avail or have you availed of this WLB initiative?

According to CIPD,[58] the take-up rates of flexible working programmes were the most frequently-used method of monitoring and evaluating WLB in organisations. Take-up rates can indicate how embedded flexible working arrangements are within an organisation. However, such data is not always a good indicator as to whether the programmes are effective.

When take-up rates alone are used to evaluate and monitor WLB, it can be difficult to demonstrate the business case for WLB programmes. Maintaining a register of the number of WLB initiative requests received initially and the number accepted or rejected can help organisations to monitor how the organisation culture supports WLB and which middle / line managers are likely to support requests from employees to avail of WLB programmes.

---

58   CIPD (2005).

Level 2: Organisational objectives

The impact of WLB policies and programmes on productivity, absenteeism, retention and recruitment can be evaluated using a variety of approaches as set out below:

What is the impact of WLB programmes on productivity?

Productivity can be measured by gathering data from weekly / monthly / yearly targets and comparing them to actual output. The levels of overtime, and the reasons for it, should also be measured. Customer satisfaction levels and complaints can also be a valuable source of information. All this information should be available from the company database supporting production, customer service and accounting processes. However, the reasons for any fall-off in productivity, increased overtime or reduced levels of customer satisfaction must be examined closely to determine whether they are related to the implementation of WLB initiatives or whether they are due to other factors.

Do WLB programmes reduce absenteeism?

Data on employee absenteeism can be obtained from the HR database. Information on the overall annual percentage of absenteeism and, in particular, self-certified days and lateness, the demographics of absentees (age profile, marital status, family commitments, job category/skills and level in the organisation) and the reasons for absenteeism should be evaluated in light of WLB programmes in operation. It is critical to examine the reasons for the absenteeism to establish whether it is linked to flexibility and / or the need for balance between work and non-work domains. When the data is analysed, it will highlight not only the costs of the absenteeism itself, but also show links to productivity, overtime and customer satisfaction levels. Where absenteeism is related to inflexibility, then WLB programmes may be useful in addressing the issue.

Do WLB programmes increase employee retention?

Data on the percentage of staff turnover, the demographics, competencies, job category and level in the organisation of each person who has terminated their employment can be obtained from the HR database. Where the information is known, it may be useful to include an indicator on the HR database to track the primary reasons employees leave the organisation.

The reason(s) for leaving the organisation can be gathered from exit interviews with a HR representative or a one-to-one meeting with the middle / line manager. However, organisations may not always obtain the real reason for termination from the employee leaving the organisation, as employees can be reluctant to give this information at the exit interview.

If employee retention is a significant problem for an organisation, it may be useful to carry out a survey / questionnaire with the person who left the organisation six months or so after the termination. This survey / questionnaire may assist in evaluating whether work-life balance and the initiatives available (or lack thereof) in the organisation were an important factor as to why they opted to leave.

Do WLB programmes assist in the employee attraction and recruitment process?

The effectiveness of recruitment campaigns can be determined by the number of vacancies to be filled in the organisation, the number of applicants for each position, the job offer / job acceptance rates, and the time taken to fill vacancies.

Good WLB policies and programmes can act as an important factor in attracting employees to an organisation and in their subsequent acceptance of job offers. When an organisation is operating in a competitive environment and needs to attract best talent, it may opt to emphasise to prospective candidates, through advertising or at interview, the cultural support for work-life balance and how the WLB initiatives are perceived within the organisation and to promote this as a compelling reason to choose the organisation.

An interview with candidates who declined the company's offer can be useful to establish the reasons for not accepting the offer and to determine whether work-life balance was an issue.

Do WLB programmes foster good employee relations?
To evaluate the link between WLB and employee relations within the organisation, a questionnaire / employee satisfaction survey can be a useful data collection tool. Statements exploring the link between employee relations and WLB can be presented and employees asked to indicate on a 5-point scale whether they agree or disagree with various statements (5 = strongly agree and 1 = strongly disagree). Statements may include:

- I really feel that my organisation respects my desire to balance work and personal / non-work demands.
- This organisation is interested in employee well-being.

Level 3: Individual Objectives
Do WLB programmes assist employees to manage their workload better?
This objective can be measured by gathering relevant data from employees using questionnaires or surveys. Employees can be asked to indicate their agreement or disagreement with various statements regarding their workload and WLB – for example:

- The WLB programmes on offer in this organisation help me to manage my workload without interfering with my personal time.
- Employees are regularly expected to put their jobs before their personal / non-work lives.
- Employees are often expected to take work home at night and / or on weekends.
- Employees on reduced hours are expected to continue to complete the same level of workload that they did while on full-time hours.

Manager / employee one-to-one feedback and / or performance appraisal also can be a useful way to obtain qualitative data and evaluate whether employees are managing their workload and finding balance in their work and personal / family domains.

Do WLB programmes lead to greater employee self-fulfilment?
Self-fulfilment can be evaluated by using a questionnaire or employee satisfaction survey. Quantitative data can be obtained by including statements linking WLB to self-fulfilment in the questionnaire / survey. Using a 5-point scale, the employee can be asked to indicate the degree to which they agree or disagree with various statements (5 = strongly agree, 1 = strongly disagree). Statements may include:

- I do not intend to be working in this organisation in a year's time, because I want to achieve a greater work-life balance.
- I am satisfied with the time and energy I have for my work and personal life.

Do WLB programmes assist in balancing work and personal / family life?
Balancing work and personal / family life can be evaluated by collecting quantitative data using an employee satisfaction survey. Data can be obtained by including statements in the questionnaire / survey, where the employee is asked to indicate the degree to which they agree or disagree with various statements (5 = strongly agree, 1 = strongly disagree). Statements can include:

- The WLB programmes on offer in this organisation help me to manage my personal and professional life better.

- My job keeps me away too much from the people and activities that are important to me.

Do WLB programmes lead to enhanced employee well-being, motivation and commitment?
Gathering and analysing data on whether employees experience a positive spill-over between work and non-work domains can determine employee well-being. This can have implications for job satisfaction, motivation and employee commitment for the individual and increased productivity and retention for the organisation.

Quantitative data can be gathered using a questionnaire. On a 5-point scale, the employee can be asked to indicate the degree to which they agree or disagree with various statements (5 = strongly agree, 1= strongly disagree). Statements can include:

- My activities at work are rewarding in, and of, themselves.

- My activities in my personal life are rewarding in, and of, themselves.

- I am motivated to work harder for this organisation because I am satisfied with my WLB.

- I am committed to staying in this organisation because I am satisfied with my WLB.

Stage 4: Linking the Findings to the Bottom Line

When the data has been gathered and analysed, as discussed in Stage 3, it can be linked to the bottom line to enable the 'value' of implementing WLB initiatives to be demonstrated in financial terms.

Table 5.4 sets out the 'hard' metrics and **Table 5.5** sets out the 'soft' measures that can be used to evaluate the impact of WLB practices at a programmatic, organisational and/or employee level. These measures can be used as a template for a systematic approach to linking the outcomes to the bottom line. At the end of phase 1 (usually six months after implementing the WLB initiative in question), it is necessary to evaluate the outcomes and compare the costs *versus* the savings / benefits associated with the WLB initiative. Finally, at the end of phase 2 (usually after 12 months), evaluation of the outcomes once again needs to be undertaken and linked to the bottom line to determine what return, if any, has been achieved on the HR investment in WLB programmes. The following is an example of how the ROI can be calculated.

Table 5.4: Linking the Hard Data Gathered & Analysed to the Bottom Line

'Hard' Metrics	Benchmark Pre-phase 1	Outcome after Phase 1 piloting: 6 months	Outcome after Phase 2: 12 months
Level 1: Programmatic metrics			
Offering WLB programmes to support the business needs of the organisation			
Up-take of WLB programmes			
Level 2: Organisational metrics			
Business outputs Productivity Customer satisfaction levels Overtime costs for employees and managers			
Reduced Absenteeism Percentage of self-certified sickness absence Lateness			
Increased retention Number of employees leaving the organisation Loss of specialised skills			
Improved Recruitment Advertising and agency costs Positions vacant versus the positions filled and time taken to fill Quality of applications received and the quality of the recruits			
Level 3: Individual metrics			
Managing the workload			
Administration Costs			

Source: Adapted from CIPD (2006b).

Table 5.5: Linking the Soft Data Gathered & Analysed to the Bottom Line

'Soft' Measures	Benchmark Pre-phase 1	Outcome after Phase 1 piloting: 6 months	Outcome after Phase 2: 12 months
Level 1: Programmatic measures			
Promotion and building awareness of WLB programmes			
Level 2: Organisational measures			
Employee relations			
Promoting a results-based culture			
Level 3: Individual measures			
Self-fulfilment for employees on and off the job			
Balancing work and personal / family life			
Employee well-being			
Motivation and commitment			

Source: Adapted from CIPD (2006b).

ROI on Retention following Implementation of WLB initiatives

Return on investment (ROI) can be calculated by evaluating the cost-benefit ratio of a particular WLB programme. ROI equals the present value of net benefits (gross benefits less costs) divided by the initial costs of the programme. The higher the benefits in relation to the costs, the greater the ROI.

To determine the ROI of a particular WLB programme on employee retention, it is necessary to calculate the percentage turnover of professional employees:

- Prior to the implementation of WLB programme.

- At the end of phase 1 (six months after the WLB programme has been implemented).

- At the end phase 2 (12 months following implementation of the WLB programme).

The net programme benefits are calculated by establishing the savings on retention (for example, reduced recruitment and selection costs as well as training and development) less the costs of implementing the WLB programme. This figure is divided by the cost of implementing the WLB programme to determine ROI.

Deloitte & Touche began measuring the savings from its formal flexible work arrangements about 10 years ago. It arrived at a figure of $41.5 million in savings by applying the standard 150% replacement multiplier to the average annual salary of workers who would have left the organisation had flexible work schedules not been an available option. The firm then multiplied those figures by the number of respondents to an internal survey who said they would have quit the firm for that reason.[59]

The qualitative data gathered and analysed can also yield desirable outcomes, such as increased employee well-being, motivation and commitment, self-fulfilment and balance in the work and non-work domains for the individuals. These outcomes can be linked to organisational outcomes such as retention, increased productivity and lower levels of absenteeism.

In addition to the cost-benefits outlined above, it is also necessary to include administration costs in relation to designing, implementing and evaluating work-life balance initiatives. These costs can include HR administration, payroll changes / administration, and management time to handle the extra workload needed for effective implementation.

Stage 5: Make Recommendations Based on the Evaluation

When the benefits of implementing WLB programmes can be quantified clearly in financial terms and shown to be greater than the costs, the HR function can make recommendations for increasing the programmes available, improving the existing programmes and / or reduction or elimination of various components not considered to be of value.

A variety of recommendations are possible as a result of monitoring and evaluating WLB programme effectiveness, including:

- A call to move towards implementing a greater array of WLB initiatives, in order to move from an inactive position on the WLB continuum to become the leader in the industry in WLB, thus delivering a competitive advantage (see **Figure 3.2**).

- Greater communication through various means to promote and build awareness of existing WLB programmes and the new programmes to be implemented.

---

[59] CIPD (2006b).

- Initiate actions to support a cultural change as the organisation moves from a 'face-time' to a 'results-oriented' culture, allowing for greater flexibility.

- Continue to monitor and evaluate WLB progress.

- Repeat the evaluation on a yearly basis and make adjustments as required.

Who Should be Involved in Monitoring & Evaluation?

This section discusses who should be involved in conducting the evaluation of the WLB initiatives. WLB initiative evaluations can take place on a number of different levels and can be operated for business units, departments, sites or on an organisation-wide basis. The key stakeholders to be involved in conducting the evaluations are set out in **Figure 5.2**.

Figure 5.2: The Stakeholders Involved in the Evaluation Process

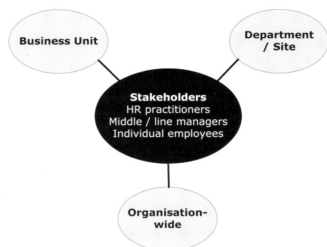

HR Practitioners / HR Function

The HR function / HR practitioners play a critical role in the overall evaluation and monitoring process of WLB policies and programmes. Ultimately, they are the custodians of WLB policy and, while a variety of stakeholders have a role to play in the practice of WLB, the HR function is responsible for ensuring that the level of monitoring and evaluation undertaken is adequate to answer the business questions regarding the efficiency and effectiveness of any WLB arrangements. A key requirement for the HR practitioner is to have the ability to engage the key stakeholders in the business to ensure that they understand the rationale behind any initiatives, their aims and objectives, and the agreed criteria in terms of measurement. When monitoring and evaluating is driven at this level, there tends to be more engagement with the process and commitment to its ultimate success.

Middle / Line Managers

Middle / line managers are the crucial link between WLB policy and WLB practice and implementation at the individual employee level. Therefore, it is important that middle / line managers not only are aware of the statutory entitlements in relation to flexible working and work-life balance, but that they understand their own company policies.

It is essential to monitor and evaluate how WLB initiatives and programmes are operated by middle / line managers. If successful implementation of WLB initiatives is to be achieved, it is vital that middle / line managers are involved in the design and formation of these initiatives from the outset. This will enable them to have a valuable input into the operation of the initiative and will contribute towards overcoming the challenges, so as to ensure that the policies are implemented successfully.

Individual / Employee

Employee feedback on WLB should be gathered in a systematic manner. Such systematic evaluations can be carried out using questionnaires / employee satisfaction surveys, performance reviews, focus groups, one-to-one feedback sessions between managers and employees (see stage 3 above). Ultimately, WLB programmes are focused at improving important employee-related outcomes and thus, employee input is essential to ensure WLB programmes are achieving their aims and objectives.

Chapter Summary

In general, organisations do not engage in systematic monitoring and evaluation of how work-life balance policies and programmes operate in practice. A comprehensive evaluation approach is necessary to determine the effectiveness of WLB programmes and to determine how they can add value to the organisation and its employees. WLB policies and programmes are viewed no longer as a means of accommodating employees; rather, they are a fundamental part of the business strategy for recruiting and retaining employees. Furthermore, WLB policies and programmes need to be an integrated part of the HR function, so that they can be viewed as an important component in the overall business strategy.

There are many challenges in implementing a systematic approach to WLB programme monitoring and evaluation, including lack of time, cumbersome evaluation systems, lack of buy-in from middle / line managers and, most importantly, lack of a link to return on investment for the organisation.

A tailored and customised approach to monitoring and evaluating WLB initiatives needs to be adopted at a programmatic, organisation and individual employee level. Accordingly, HR practitioners need to convince senior management of the return on the investment in WLB to ensure continued commitment and investment.

6: Organisational Consequences & Outcomes of WLB Policies & Programmes

This chapter describes the benefits and challenges that accrue to organisations in the adoption and implementation of WLB initiatives.

First, the benefits of operating WLB programmes are discussed and considered. The advantages of WLB initiatives identified in the 2007 Work-Life Balance in Ireland study are compared and contrasted with findings from other international studies. The purpose of highlighting these advantages is to provide encouragement to organisations that otherwise might be cautious or anxious about the implementation of such initiatives. Building awareness of the positive benefits that organisations can expect in return for their investment in WLB initiatives may go some way towards alleviating these anxieties. The chapter also outlines how organisations can encourage greater uptake of WLB programmes by employees.

Then the chapter focuses on some of the challenges that can emerge in the adoption and implementation of WLB programmes. This book is a practitioner guide to the implementation of WLB initiatives and, therefore, it would be remiss not to address the challenges often faced by organisations in this regard. In doing so, the intention is to share the experiences of other organisations in the hope that these will provide both insights into problems encountered and solutions to those challenges.

Benefits for Organisations from Operating Work-Life Balance Programmes

There are many potential benefits from designing and implementing WLB programmes and initiatives effectively. Numerous well-known organisations report positive outcomes as a result of their WLB policies:[60]

- Xerox UK estimates that it has saved over stg£1 million in the last 5 years through **enhanced retention** as a result of its improved work-life balance policies.

- Goldman Sachs and BT report a **higher rate of women returning to work** after maternity leave, as a result of implementing WLB policies. These measures include post-maternity-leave arrangements and establishing a new mothers' network. BT estimates that it saved stg£3 million in recruitment costs alone, due to the initiatives in the year to March 2003.

- Penguin Publishing has cut its **absenteeism rates** to 2.4%, compared to the industry average of 4.8%, by providing a generous range of WLB policies.

Such desirable outcomes from these international organisations provide a compelling argument for the introduction and management of WLB programmes.

In the Irish context, a number of benefits resulting from the operation of WLB programmes were identified in the *2007 Work-Life Balance in Ireland* study and are presented in **Figure 6.1**. Each of these benefits will be discussed in more detail below.

Figure 6.1: The Reported Benefits of Work-Life Balance Programmes

---

60   Poelmans & Sahibzada (2004).

Various stakeholders in the organisation have the potential to focus on different aspects of HR policies. Thus, it is important to understand whether management and employees report the same benefits from work-life balance programmes. If organisations are to truly achieve the benefits set out in **Figure 6.1** above, then employees, middle / line managers, and senior management should all share the same view as to the reality of these benefits.

In an effort to explore these multi-stakeholder perceptions, the *2007 Work-Life Balance in Ireland* study explored the perceptions of HR directors / managers, middle / line managers and employees in relation to the positive effects of implementing work-life balance programmes. **Table 6.1** presents the percentage of respondents agreeing or disagreeing with a number of statements regarding the beneficial effects of implementing work-life balance policies and programmes in their organisations.

Table 6.1: The Positive Effects of Work-Life Balance Policies & Programmes – Multi-Stakeholder Comparison

Statement included in the survey	HR directors / managers		Middle / line managers		Employees	
	Agree	Disagree	Agree	Disagree	Agree	Disagree
WLB policies and programmes foster good employee relations	80%	20%	96%	4%	89%	11%
WLB policies and programmes increase productivity	87%	13%	81%	17%	81%	15%
WLB policies and programmes reduce absenteeism	93%	7%	89%	9%	84%	13%
WLB policies and programmes lower staff turnover	93%	7%	94%	6%	76%	17%
WLB policies and programmes positively impact on recruitment and retention	93%	7%	96%	4%	86%	10%
WLB policies and programmes improve staff motivation and commitment	100%	0%	90%	10%	84%	13%

Source: 2007 Work-Life Balance in Ireland *study.*

The data in this study shows that only nominal differences exist across the various stakeholders in the organisations in relation to the perception of the effects of work-life balance policies and programmes. Both management and employees share strong views that implementing work-life balance policies and programmes have positive consequences for the organisation. This consistency reassures us that the views of management, who are sometimes accused of being removed from the reality of the employee workplace experiences, are aligned with those of employees.

Detailed semi-structured interviews were undertaken with a number of HR and middle / line managers to probe further the perceived advantages of implementing WLB initiatives. As a result, a significant amount of qualitative data was gathered, including ample anecdotal evidence of the benefits of such initiatives. **Panel 6.1** shows extracts from these interviews, which provide strong support for the findings of the quantitative data outlined in **Table 6.1** above.

We now explore in more detail each of the six benefits of WLB programmes as reported by HR directors, middle management, and employees.

1. Job Satisfaction

The findings highlighted in **Table 6.1** indicate clearly that organisations perceive that WLB initiatives are effective in raising the level of job satisfaction among their employees. Moreover, enhanced job satisfaction leads to increased levels of motivation and commitment among employees, improved rates of retention as well as lower absenteeism. Indeed, the link between these organisational processes can be seen as direct, indirect and, importantly, reciprocal in nature, as evidenced in **Figure 6.1**.

Job satisfaction remains one of the most influential concepts in modern organisations. According to psychologists,[61] the main factors that affect job satisfaction are mentally-challenging work, equitable rewards, supportive working conditions and supportive colleagues. It is quite evident that the supportive context of organisations that offer WLB programmes contributes hugely to raising levels of job satisfaction. Specifically, work scheduling or flexi-time is said to be particularly valuable in this regard. In having the option to work flexible hours, employees can balance personal needs and work effectiveness more easily. It also fosters a sense of pride among employees that they are valuable to the organisation and that management is concerned about their welfare.

One of the key reasons why job satisfaction has such a strong impact on so many other aspects of employees' behaviour is because of people's innate sense of fairness.[62] Employees very quickly will leave an organisation / job, or reduce their effort, if they feel their contributions are not being recognised and valued appropriately. The perceived fairness of

---

[61] George & Jones (2007).
[62] Bowman *et al.* (2006).

the exchange is the crucial factor. In the past, most employees felt treated fairly if they earned a certain salary and were offered promotional opportunities. Currently, however, one of the most highly-sought-after outcomes is balance between the various domains of life. The extent to which the workforce of tomorrow achieves this balance will influence their levels of job satisfaction, with all its ensuing repercussions. Indeed, work-life imbalance has been found to be a major factor in work dissatisfaction, which leads to a number of other withdrawal behaviours, including staff turnover and non-genuine sick absence.[63]

Research has demonstrated that the existence of WLB programmes is positively related to organisational commitment and job satisfaction, regardless of whether employees had availed of or participated in these programmes.[64] This suggests that introducing such work-life balance policies demonstrates the organisation's concern for employee well-being and, consequently, raises morale and job satisfaction all-round.

2. Productivity

In the *2007 Work-Life Balance in Ireland* study, the impact of WLB programmes on productivity was viewed as positive. This is interesting, since many commentators argue that the introduction of work-life balance programmes, particularly those that reduce working hours, has deleterious effects on productivity.

Certainly, effective management of WLB programmes is important to ensure that there is adequate staff coverage to achieve the goals and objectives of the organisation. Due to the simultaneous needs of ensuring continuity of service and facilitating the participation of employees in WLB initiatives, a certain degree of cross-training and employee flexibility has occurred in many of the organisations that participated in the *2007 Work-Life Balance in Ireland* study (see **Panel 6.2**). As employees' skills increase, they can move more easily between jobs to fill gaps and can derive the benefits that such job movement brings. These advantages include raised levels of job satisfaction and motivation, which positively affect the quality of working life for those concerned. Also significant is the fact that cross-training may improve the possibility of workers helping one another or sharing their workload. Furthermore, multi-skilling can be advantageous, as it results in employees receiving a variety of work, which can lead to potential career development opportunities.

Panel 6.2: Multi-skilling & Cross-Training

"The organisation needs to multi-skill its employees and therefore have a more multi-skilled workforce resulting in greater flexibility among employees." - Middle manager, Pharmaceutical sector

"Managing work-sharing has its own benefits – we can move employees around – resulting in greater flexibility and multi-skilled employees." - HR manager, Public sector

"WLB programmes allow for the development of expertise in the organisation in that such programmes enhance the organisation's ability to retain employees for longer periods of time." - Middle manager, Telecommunications sector

Source: 2007 *Work-Life Balance in Ireland* study.

---

[63] Hughes & Bozionelos (2007).
[64] Scandura & Lankau (1997).

3. Employee Retention

Irish organisations have made the link between WLB programmes and enhanced retention rates. It appears that, as employees perceive that the organisation is responsive to their needs, they are less likely to seek out alternative employment. High retention rates reduce turnover costs. This can result in increased productivity, where it is combined with higher levels of job satisfaction. It is interesting to note that elevated retention rates have also been found to be strongly-related to high customer loyalty and greater profitability.[65]

The costs of employee turnover are significant, as a senior manager at the ESB comments:

> "… when an employee opts out of the organisation, there is a huge amount of knowledge and experience that can be wasted".

Staff turnover is estimated to cost the US economy $5 trillion annually. Reducing turnover is a key concern. High levels of staff turnover create major costs for the organisation. Even the replacement costs for one employee can be quite substantial. The recruitment procedure, involving advertising, shortlisting, interviewing and associated administration, can be extremely costly. New recruits will require induction, in particular retraining, which eats further into organisational budgets. In addition, the loss of specialised skills can also lead to a reduction in productivity.

The implementation of WLB initiatives may be crucial in giving an organisation a competitive edge in the quest for the most talented staff. The extent to which companies engage in talent management, and feature WLB initiatives as a relevant tool to support it, reflect better management practices and act as a distinguishing feature of excellent organisations.

WLB policies have the potential to form a significant part of an imaginative talent management process that operates to hold onto the key employees that drive the success of their operations. When executives devote between 20% and 40% of their time to talent management because they believe it is the best means for securing competitive advantage,[66] organisations need to develop a 'talent mindset', in which the importance of holding onto key organisational members is kept to the forefront of its objectives. The retention of skilled female working mothers is particularly challenging. However, organisations can retain some of these staff by implementing flexible working practices that suit personal and work time demands.

4. Employee Attraction

One of the main advantages to organisations of providing supportive WLB initiatives is the ability to attract high-performing candidates with the necessary skills and competences. The workplace is becoming increasingly competitive and the ability to build a strong employer brand image as an 'employer of choice' has the potential to increase significantly an organisation's competitive advantage through attracting high calibre employees.

It was the view of the majority of participating organisations in the *2007 Work-Life Balance in Ireland* study, that certain WLB initiatives helped them to attract candidates to their organisation. They saw WLB programmes as a valuable recruitment tool. Additionally, they felt that many employees not only make themselves aware of the extent to which an organisation is supportive of WLB, but also allow this information to influence

---

[65]   Eisenberger *et al.* (2002).

[66]   McCauley & Wakefield (2006).

their decisions when seeking and accepting an employment offer. The following quotation from a HR manager in the pharmaceutical sector underscores this point:

> "Supporting WLB helps our brand in terms of recruitment and gives us a competitive advantage."

A company brand is used to gain customer loyalty and to increase profits through market differentiation. Similarly, an employer brand can be used to build a unique set of attributes and qualities that differentiate it from competitors when it comes to what it can offer potential employees. Although this set of attributes is often intangible, it can make an organisation distinctive, whereby it promises a particular kind of employment experience, and appeals to prospective candidates who should perform to their best in its culture.[67]

This branding process can be deployed by organisations to compete more effectively in the labour market and to drive employee loyalty through effective recruitment, engagement and retention policies. Ensuring that the external promise of your employer brand matches the internal reality of what it is like to work in the organisation is central to the successful operation of the branding process as a retention tool.

There are eight steps to creating an employer brand, in which the organisation's commitment to WLB practices can be sold to potential employees (see **Figure 6.2**).[68]

Numerous Irish-based companies have generated a WLB brand. Organisations with strong WLB initiatives are recognised in the list of the 50 Best Companies to Work for in Ireland, produced each year by the Great Place to Work Institute and published by the *Irish Independent*. For instance, in 2007, Airtricity secured the 'Best Company Overall Award' and Premier Group was awarded 'Best Practice for Work-Life Balance'. Being listed as one of the best companies to work for is an invaluable tool when trying to attract highly-talented individuals.

5. Employee Well-Being

Employee well-being is gaining increasing importance in the quest for effective human resource management practice. Satisfactory work-life balance is one of the factors that contributes to employee well-being at work, by reducing stress. Organisations in the *2007 Work-Life Balance in Ireland* study stated very clearly that they felt the presence of WLB initiatives was central in reducing levels of stress among employees. Some work-life balance programmes, such as flexi-time, can assist employees in balancing their personal and family demands with their work. This reduces stress and conflict.

There is little doubt that, on a global scale, levels of workplace stress continue to rise. The World Health Organisation[69] has expressed concern over the negative consequences of stress for individuals' psychological well-being, organisational performance, and financial costs to organisations. Although an array of contributory factors are said to have precipitated this rise in stress levels, attention is drawn increasingly to the relative contributions of work and non-work factors to psychological ill-health. It is clear that combining a job that requires high levels of input on the part of the employee with the demands of family life can be particularly challenging for some employees. If the organisation does not provide WLB initiatives that will enable the employee to better manage these demands, it is likely that stress and burnout will be the eventual outcome.

---

[67] CIPD (2007e).

[68] Adapted from Backhaus & Tikoo (2004).

[69] World Health Organisation (2001).

Figure 6.2: Building a WLB Brand

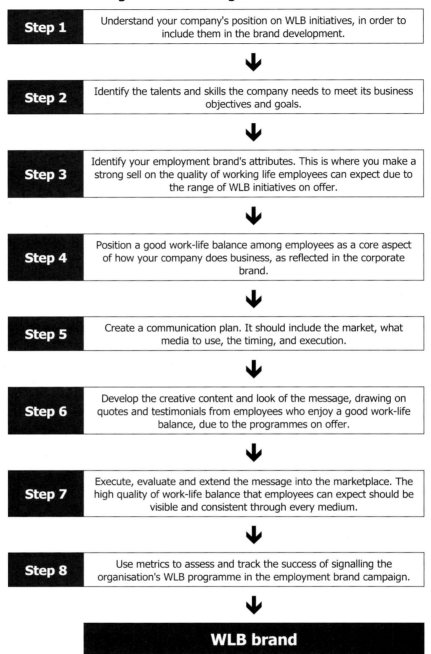

Step 1	Understand your company's position on WLB initiatives, in order to include them in the brand development.
Step 2	Identify the talents and skills the company needs to meet its business objectives and goals.
Step 3	Identify your employment brand's attributes. This is where you make a strong sell on the quality of working life employees can expect due to the range of WLB initiatives on offer.
Step 4	Position a good work-life balance among employees as a core aspect of how your company does business, as reflected in the corporate brand.
Step 5	Create a communication plan. It should include the market, what media to use, the timing, and execution.
Step 6	Develop the creative content and look of the message, drawing on quotes and testimonials from employees who enjoy a good work-life balance, due to the programmes on offer.
Step 7	Execute, evaluate and extend the message into the marketplace. The high quality of work-life balance that employees can expect should be visible and consistent through every medium.
Step 8	Use metrics to assess and track the success of signalling the organisation's WLB programme in the employment brand campaign.

WLB brand

Source: Adapted from Backhaus & Tikoo (2004).

Organisations need to be encouraged to recognise the direct and indirect link between healthy WLB practices and organisational improvements. A healthy workplace is one where the employees' needs for personal and professional well-being are integrated satisfactorily with the organisation's objectives for profitability and productivity. Given the enormous financial and human costs associated with unhealthy organisations, any processes or programmes that build psychological and physical well-being in the organisation are to be welcomed. It is evident that the broad array of work-life balance programmes available (as outlined in **Chapter 4**) are a means of enhancing employee well-being.

6. Good Employee Relations

WLB initiatives foster good employee relations. It enables the employee to feel valued, not only from the point of view of productivity, but also in relation to their other priorities outside of the work sphere. It casts the manager and organisation in a supportive role, accommodating the personal issues of their workers, while, at the same time, ensuring that targets are reached. WLB programmes also may result in employees feeling comfortable in bringing up personal or family issues at work.

In terms of worker well-being, availing of WLB programmes reduces the level of stress experienced by some employees as they attempt to reconcile demands from home and their job. This, in turn, leads to increased mental health and corresponding lower levels of stress and burnout. They also experience less work-family conflict and are more satisfied with their lives. This impacts positively on staff morale and may lead to improved quality of relationships between employees.

WLB programmes have been shown to foster higher levels of motivation among staff, as they feel the organisation is supporting their home life. They also foster a sense of control over one's life in that employees can seek out WLB initiatives that will enable them to manage both their work and personal commitments. Furthermore, WLB programmes increase employee loyalty to the organisation, reducing the need for costly recruitment and training of employees. Thus, WLB initiatives lead to staff being significantly more satisfied with their jobs, more committed to the organisation and more likely to remain with their employer.

Factors that Influence the Likelihood of Employees Availing of WLB Initiatives

It is often the case that making various WLB programmes available to employees does not translate into significant uptake by employees of these programmes. Many factors affect whether employees actually use the WLB programmes available in the organisation. If organisations are to accrue the benefits outlined above, it is important to ensure that employees feel that they can avail of the various WLB policies and programmes available. In broad terms, there are a number of approaches organisations can adopt to encourage employees in the uptake of WLB initiatives including:

- Making sure that suitable programmes are available to meet employee needs and requirements.
- Ensuring ease of access to programmes.
- Promotion of positive and successful outcomes in the operation of the programmes (for example, by reference to case studies and role models).
- Increased awareness and communication of the programmes available.
- Ensuring line manager / supervisor support for using WLB programmes.
- Colleague support for using WLB programmes is present.

Handling requests from employees to avail of WLB initiatives seriously, as well as ensuring that the policies are implemented in a fair and equitable manner, can increase significantly the likelihood of employees using WLB initiatives. Specific and practical day-to-day approaches that organisations should attempt to develop in order to encourage employee uptake of WLB programmes include:

- **Publicise successes:** Feature managers using flexible schedules as success stories in company communications. Ensure that, where a WLB initiative has been successful, it is celebrated and communicated. Useful lessons can be derived, and training developed for managers and co-workers, from such successes.

- **Keep lines of communication open:** Try to encourage an open approach for staff to discuss problems or issues they are facing in their personal life. Adopt a joint problem-solving approach, whereby both manager and employee are jointly responsible for proposing solutions to WLB problems.

- **Challenge management to self-assess the degree to which there is a 'bravado mentality' within their section:** How do they contribute to the long hours culture? Challenge the perception that long hours are required in order to meet organisational goals.

- **Include presentations on work-life balance during new employee orientation sessions and career development for all employees.**

Traditionally, women managers have tended to avail of WLB programmes more often than men. However, there are a number of practices that can promote greater gender equity in the use of WLB:

- Promote use of programmes for multiple purposes, not only for child-rearing.
- Run focus groups to find out why men are reluctant to use the programmes.
- Present family-friendly policies as meeting business needs, not as interrupting them.

Some managers may need a little convincing that WLB initiatives are 'worth the pain'. For that reason, the benefits of WLB programmes need to be established clearly, as follows:

- Collect hard data on WLB policies and programmes that can be used to demonstrate the 'value' of the initiatives for employee well-being and how they can support the business needs of the organisation. For example, studies might compare stress-related health care costs, staff turnover, and absenteeism among workers in units where high levels of managerial support for WLB initiatives exist.

- Additional comparisons can be made using measures of customer satisfaction, hours of coverage, number of customers served per hour, and the degree to which employees go the extra mile for the organisation or other team members without being asked.

- Encourage managers to experiment with different work schedules and hours on a trial basis in departments. Such piloting of programmes can help managers to see whether they are feasible and can change attitudes towards their use.

Finally, research[70] indicates that it is worth promoting the fact that, at times, work and family lives actually enrich each other. When an individual can integrate their work and family domains successfully, the 'synergy' derived from this experience can result in a high sense of well-being for them. In fact, satisfaction with work and family have been found to raise individuals' levels of happiness, life satisfaction and perceived quality of life.

---

[70] Greenhaus & Powell (2006).

Furthermore, experiencing work-family enrichment may come about due to the buffering effect that family roles can offer to protect individuals from distress they may experience in work roles. The energy that employees derive from positive experiences in one role can serve to motivate behaviour in other roles.

Challenges in Operating Work-Life Balance Policies & Programmes

The potential benefits of introducing WLB initiatives are undeniable; however, many organisations experience considerable challenges in doing so. These obstacles include:

- Managing the workload in a competitive and demanding environment *versus* managing the need of employees for greater flexibility.
- Managerial resistance.
- Ensuring fairness and equality in terms of access and eligibility.

1. Managing the Workload

Some work-life balance programmes inevitably mean a reduction in working hours for those availing of them (for example, part-time working, job-sharing, career breaks). The primary objective for any organisation is to meet its targets, irrespective of employee work schedules and patterns. The main challenges of managing the workload in the context of WLB programmes include:

- Ensuring sufficient staff resources to provide service to customers.
- Making sure appropriate skill requirements are available at all times.
- Co-ordinating different work schedules.
- Enabling smooth transitions between employees involved in alternative work schedules.
- Providing appropriate facilities to accommodate employees on alternative work schedules.

The *2007 Work-Life Balance in Ireland* study examined the perceptions of HR directors / managers, middle / line managers and employees of the challenges in implementing and managing WLB programmes. The findings are presented in **Table 6.2** and **Panel 6.3**.

When compared to HR directors / managers and employees, middle / line managers more strongly agree that the negative effects of introducing WLB initiatives were shortages of staff at key times and increased managerial workloads. These factors in organisations directly affect the middle / line managers' roles and responsibilities.

**Table 6.2: The Challenges of Work-Life Balance Policies &
Programmes – Multi-Stakeholder Comparison**

Statement included in study	HR directors / managers		Middle / line managers		Employees	
	Agree	Disagree	Agree	Disagree	Agree	Disagree
WLB policies and programmes lead to shortages of staff at key times	40%	60%	62%	37%	55%	36%
WLB policies and programmes increase managerial workloads	73%	27%	72%	28%	50%	39%
WLB policies and programmes increase overall costs of the business	40%	47%	47%	46%	42%	41%

Source: 2007 Work-Life balance in Ireland *study.*

**Panel 6.3: The Challenges of Work-Life Balance Policies
& Programmes – Multi-Stakeholder Comparison**

The perceived challenges in implementing WLB initiatives were explored further with HR directors / managers and middle / line managers during interviews. The following quotations are representative of the findings from the *2007 Work-Life Balance in Ireland* study:

"As a small business unit, it can be difficult to operate work-life balance policies and programmes ... such programmes can put pressure on meeting deadlines with a limited pool of resources." - Line manager, Manufacturing sector

"The department that I work in is the most 'measured' place in the organisation – we need to know how many calls have been received – phones need to be manned at all times – we cannot control the number of calls we receive on a daily basis. Therefore, making sure we have enough staff on at all times is a challenge." - HR manager, Telecommunications sector.

Source: 2007 Work-Life Balance in Ireland *study.*

---

2. Managerial Attitude & Resistance

The attitude of managers in relation to employee participation in WLB programmes sends a very powerful message and plays a critical role in WLB success.[71] The manner in which they communicate in relation to the initiatives, and the ease with which they implement WLB practices into their departments, is central to employees' tendency to engage with the practices.

The need for 'chameleonic' managers, who readily adapt to the changing work environment, has never been more evident. Not only are they required to devise new ways of thinking about and performing their role, but they must also assume a greater co-ordinating role than before. The range of atypical workers who form part of most managers' direct responsibility is increasing and so too, therefore, are the requirements for managers to integrate those workers fully into the performance environment.

---

[71] Kossek, Barber & Winters (1999).

Generating a smooth workflow, for example, incorporating the efforts of multiple lone e-workers or tele-workers by deploying cutting-edge technology will become a critical competence of modern-day managers. A dispersed and diverse workforce creates a bigger demand on managers to build a sense of community within their unit. This process rests on balancing their coaching and facilitating repertoire of skills, with their planning, organising, and controlling skills. For example, it may be necessary for managers to protect those who are engaging in tele-working from colleagues' accusations that they do not have an equal share of the workload. In addition, line managers may be required to influence staff to accept unconventional modes of working and to emphasise the significant benefits of such approaches. Moreover, managers may have to rely on their supporting skills as they aid their staff in overcoming demanding home and work commitments.

A number of skills are required to enable managers to manage WLB effectively. First, team-building skills are required, to ensure a cohesive staff unit is maintained, despite the fact that some employees may be isolated from the main worksite or working different schedules. Participative decision-making will need to be fostered, so that the needs of those who are availing of WLB initiatives and those who are not have equal input into decisions that affect their staff unit. Managers also need to be equipped to deal with conflict that may arise from WLB programmes, such as confusion over ownership of tasks between colleagues who are job-sharing the same work role. Moreover, supervisors need to be effective communicators, to explain the requirements of various WLB initiatives. Negotiating agreement and commitment among staff in terms of varying schedules, task allocation and deadlines is crucial to ensure productivity is maintained, and that WLB programmes are implemented correctly. Time management and dealing with employee stress levels are additional key managerial skills necessary for WLB policy operation – for example, to negotiate a large variety of work schedules and suggest appropriate WLB programmes to combat some employees' levels of stress. In a similar vein, managers must pay attention to the productivity levels of their employees to ensure a productive work environment is maintained, despite flexible working conditions.

Furthermore, if managers themselves do not avail of WLB practices, they send a strong message concerning the incompatibility of career advancement with such initiatives. Managers may not do so because of the risk of being perceived to be less work- / career-focused. However, if managers themselves use some of the WLB initiatives on offer, they communicate a clear message that it is acceptable to place personal time-demands on an equal footing with work time-demands.

Senior management attitudes towards WLB may also pose a challenge. For instance, they may perceive WLB programmes as leading to reduced productivity and creating staffing problems. However, their attitudes are pivotal to ensuring the success of WLB programmes and how they are viewed throughout the organisation. Therefore, if resistance towards WLB policies is present, the numerous long-term advantages of these initiatives should be emphasised to senior management. The reduction in staff turnover costs, increase in job satisfaction and motivation, coupled with the positive effect of WLB programmes on employee relations as well as public relations, are some of the benefits that could be highlighted.

As one HR manager in the public sector noted:

"WLB has to be driven from the top and has to be part of what the senior people do themselves. If all senior people work 60 hours per week and working long hours becomes the norm … then it is hard to believe that WLB is an integral part of the organisation".

3. Equity and Fairness

Given the realities of the business context, there will be limitations and constraints in terms of the number and type of employees who can avail of any particular WLB programme within an organisation. It is important, therefore, that decisions relating to access and eligibility are fair and consistent across different managers. In the past, many work-life balance programmes focused on employees with childcare responsibilities. However, focusing WLB on a certain cohort of staff (for example, working parents) can lead to discontent and perceived favouritism towards those employees who have childcare duties. It is important that both male and female employees perceive that they have equal accessibility to WLB initiatives. In addition, staff should feel that these programmes are open to all.

Many organisations have policies and guidelines that managers / supervisors can follow when making WLB decisions. Yet, not all issues will be covered by such documentation. If a company has not already set out its approach to managing a particular WLB issue, individual managers have to make a judgement on how to proceed; inevitably, this can lead to challenges in consistency and fairness. While managers may have the best will in the world in relation to resolving the WLB matter for an employee, his / her decision and action may be perceived as arbitrary when viewed in relation to the actions of other managers in similar situations. The eight-stage model presented in this book provides a useful framework to help organisations design, implement and manage WLB policies and programmes in a fairer and more equitable manner.

Because equity and fairness are such significant issues in people management, some companies consider them at the design stage of the WLB programme. For example, at Procter & Gamble, a basic operating principle is that *any* WLB initiative an employee wants to use is explored and negotiated between an employee and his / her supervisor. The purpose of this exploration and negotiation is to establish whether the initiative is both beneficial for the individual and not too disruptive for the business.

Application procedures need to be transparent, with a well-established and documented process, to ensure that the standards and reasons for granting access to WLB to certain individuals are consistent and open to scrutiny. The perceptions of employees who are unable to avail of WLB practices need to be carefully managed, so that resentment does not build up between colleagues.

Managers should promote awareness of the wide variety of WLB options available and encourage employees to avail of the WLB practices they are eligible for. Managers also should make sure that those who do not avail of WLB programmes do not carry the workload for employees availing of such initiatives. This could be achieved by managers monitoring task allocation and completion rates among all staff. Structures also could be put in place for employees to air their grievances if they feel workloads are being unfairly distributed, due to WLB workplace arrangements. A number of options are available to organisations to overcome the challenge of inequity and unfairness in terms of WLB access, eligibility and management:

- **Establish flexibility as a norm:** Often the biggest stumbling block managers have to deal with is perceptions among employees that all are contributing equally to work output. It is normal that employees compare their contribution to group processes and performance with that of other colleagues. Problems can arise when inequity is perceived. It is important that employees who are working reduced hours are not perceived to be contributing proportionately less compared with those working full-time. Given that WLB programmes are an integral aspect of organisational processes and functions, groups need to spend some time re-negotiating a shared understanding of what is a 'just' or 'fair' contribution. Work teams / groups need to come together and discuss relative contributions that allow for differences in amount, timing, and place of work. There needs to be acceptance of an agreement with the team's definition of equitable performance, in full recognition that low visibility is not construed as a lack of commitment, contribution or capability.

- **Personal interaction:** Managers could encourage off-site personnel to spend some time with their colleagues outside of team meetings. Organisations need to consider alternative and appropriate forums to facilitate personal interaction and networking between employees. As a social camaraderie develops between members, differences in workload, work schedule, and work location become less salient.

- **Pro-active availability:** Managers could encourage those employees who are participating in WLB programmes to be pro-active in contacting their colleagues in relation to workload. Pro-active efforts on behalf of such workers send a message to standard work-week employees of commitment and motivation. This also reduces uncertainty concerning the integrity of their involvement in work projects.

Chapter Summary

Drawing on the 2007 Work-Life Balance in Ireland *study, this chapter explored the benefits and challenges associated with implementing and managing work-life balance initiatives in organisations. The effective management of work-life balance can accrue benefits for the organisation, such as reducing absenteeism, lowering employee turnover, increasing staff motivation and commitment, and fostering good employee relations. The benefits for employees include increased job satisfaction and increased employee well-being.*

Notwithstanding these benefits, there are inevitable challenges that must be overcome in managing work-life balance strategy, policy and practice. If a significant proportion of the workforce avail of flexible working options, especially those that reduce working hours, such as job-sharing, work-sharing, part-time working, and term-time working, managing the workload with reduced working hours is a challenge for organisations and management. Furthermore, managerial resistance, particularly at line management level, can be a barrier to the effective implementation and management of work-life balance practices, because of the perceived increase in administration associated with managing workers on WLB or flexible arrangements.

Ensuring there is fairness and equality in terms of access to, and eligibility for, various WLB programmes is also a key consideration for organisations adopting these arrangements.

The chapter also highlighted that offering a broad array of WLB programmes does not necessarily mean employees can avail of these programmes easily. A number of factors can act as a deterrent to the use of WLB arrangements, such as lack of colleague or supervisory support and perceived negative career consequences, and so these issues need to be managed at a management and organisational level.

7: Conclusion & Future Directions

T his chapter reviews some of the key work-life balance issues for management and organisations addressed in this book.

WLB areas for improvement as identified by employees in the 2007 Work-Life Balance in Ireland *study are presented.*

The chapter concludes by identifying some of the issues at national and EU level likely to impact the work-life balance agenda into the future.

Work-Life Balance – Key Issues for Managers & Organisations

The purpose of this book is to provide managers and organisations with a guide to design, deliver, manage and evaluate work-life balance policies and programmes effectively and successfully at enterprise level. Drawing on the findings of the *2007 Work-Life Balance in Ireland* study, as well as a review of key publications and policy developments in the area, we now present a summary of the implications of WLB initiatives for organisations and management.

The main issue for organisations is that the focus on WLB and the increasing requests from employees for greater work-life balance practices is likely to be a central concern of the modern enterprise, due to a range of individual, social and environmental factors. Although organisations may be hesitant in introducing WLB policies and programmes, due to concerns over costs, control and operational issues, a strong business case can be made for the implementation of WLB initiatives. The benefits include enhanced levels of employee well-being, attendance and retention, higher morale and commitment among staff and increased levels of productivity. Moreover, the presence of a suite of WLB programmes can attract potential employees and help with the organisation's public profile as an employer of choice. In order to accrue these benefits, organisations should take certain steps to encourage employees to avail of WLB programmes, where they are available. Such actions include publicising successful features of the WLB programme, presenting them as contributing to business objectives and promoting the relevance of WLB programmes for all staff, and not only for women and child-rearing purposes.

Despite these benefits, challenges to successful WLB programmes remain. Organisations will need to devote particular effort to deal with these issues, bearing in mind that changing the mindset and culture regarding work-life balance can be challenging. The 8-stage model of WLB design, implementation and evaluation presented in **Figure 1.1** and explored throughout this book should assist organisations in the management of work-life balance. Organisations must determine what set of WLB programmes and initiatives is suitable for the organisation. This will be influenced by the work-life balance strategy the organisation wants to adopt, as well as the business needs and employee demands for WLB initiatives. A critical aspect of effective work-life balance implementation is consultation and communication with the key stakeholders involved, who include senior managers, middle / line managers, employees, and relevant employee representative groups. While there is a range of WLB options to choose from, not all will suit each individual organisation or, indeed, be required by its employees. The WLB initiatives adopted and implemented by the organisation may change over time as the needs and requirements of those concerned evolve. It is important, therefore, to ensure regular monitoring and evaluation of WLB programmes to allow changes and improvements to be made where necessary.

The main issue for management with respect to WLB programmes is their ability to implement and manage work-life balance policies and programmes. Managerial support for WLB has been found to be a critical factor in determining WLB effectiveness at the employee level. Managers need to reflect on the key role they play in the operation of work-life balance and consider how they can support employee work-life balance demands and expectations. An important issue for managers is determining employee eligibility to avail of WLB initiatives. Managers need to focus attention on the process by which requests for participation in WLB programmes are submitted, and the manner in which decisions are made. Training managers and staff involved in the design, management and evaluation of

WLB is an important predictor of successful WLB management practice. Such training could incorporate educating managers about the WLB policies and practices in operation in the organisation; training on how to manage WLB requests and the criteria to use to grant, refuse, or postpone employee requests to avail of particular WLB initiatives; and establishing and explaining the business case for WLB programmes. Managers also need to be closely involved in the monitoring and evaluation of WLB programmes to ensure their value and effectiveness in meeting the needs of all those concerned. Evaluation of the outcomes and productivity of those engaging in WLB practices is an important process to ensure performance targets, objectives and goals are met.

Looking to the Future: Employee Demands & Expectations

Employee demands and expectations have been identified as one of the catalysts in the growth of work-life balance as a key workplace issue. Employees in both the private and public sectors increasingly are calling for greater flexibility in terms of working time and place of work. Where flexi-time is in operation, employees are calling for greater access for all staff, as well as extending the core hours of work. Employees are also calling for greater opportunities to tele-work or e-work. In the private sector, some employees would like the opportunity to work a compressed working week (for example, working four 10-hour days rather than working five eight-hour days). In the public sector, term-time working is a popular initiative available to employees with school-going children. There are calls for a similar initiative to be made available to all staff, regardless of childcare responsibilities. Other improvement areas identified by employees include adequate staffing to ensure workloads are not increased due to flexible working arrangements and greater access to, and support for those engaging in, WLB initiatives.

Employees who participated in the *2007 Work-Life Balance in Ireland* study were asked how their organisation might improve work-life balance policies, practices and opportunities in their organisation. **Table 7.1** presents the responses from employees in the private and public sectors in rank order of those most commonly cited.

What is clear from the findings outlined in **Table 7.1** is that there is now an increasing awareness among employees of the importance of getting the balance correct between work and the non-work domains of life. In line with this growing awareness, employee expectations are also increasing in terms of the role they expect their employer to play in assisting them achieve this balance. While many organisations have been making tentative steps towards addressing the work-life balance concerns of employees, evidence from this study suggests that there is still room for improvement.

For both public and private sector employees, the top three areas for improvement identified centred on challenging the structure of how individuals work. It is clear that employees have increasing expectations and requirements for greater flexibility as to how, when and where they work. Advances in technology have made it possible for individuals to work from almost anywhere, at almost any time – as a result, we are likely to see organisations moving towards harnessing this technological capability to satisfy employee demands, with a view to increasing productivity, while potentially reducing costs.

Table 7.1: The Future of Work-Life Balance: Areas for Improvement Identified by Employees

Private Sector	Public Sector
1. Flexi-time Introduce a flexi-time system. Make it a formal arrangement, open and transparent. Increase availability to all employees.	**1. Flexi-time** Improve the existing flexi-time system. Expand the core hours to 7am – 7pm to facilitate commuting / traffic. Increase availability to all grades.
2. Home-working and Tele-working Increase opportunities to employees to avail of home-working / tele-working. Support the associated costs (for example, phone and broadband).	**2. Home-working & Tele-working** Increase opportunities to employees to avail of home-working / tele-working in particular in roles which can be easily facilitated.
3. Compressed working week Allow employees to work longer days, allowing one day off (for example, four 10-hour days per week rather than five eight-hour days).	**3. Term-time working** Make term-time working or a similar programme available to all employees - not just those with childcare responsibilities.
4. Increase staff resources To reduce workloads and long hours.	**4. Increase staff resources** Ensure employees on WLB / flexible practices are replaced to reduce individual workloads for employees not availing of flexible practices.
5. Childcare support Crèche on-site or subsidised nursery places outside of work.	**5. Childcare support** Greater facilities to assist employees manage childcare, either in the workplace or in external facilities.
6. Access Increase access to employees to avail of WLB / flexible practices.	
7. Support Greater understanding and support by senior management towards employees to avail of WLB / flexible practices.	

Both public and private sector employees identified flexi-time as the first potential improvement that organisations could look to in order to improve the working lives of their employees. The recommendations from employees with regard to flexi-time tend to focus around the improvement of existing schemes, so that they are open and transparent, and their extension to all employees. In addition, employees in the public sector were keen to see the core working hours extended, to allow employees even greater flexibility in terms of when they work. The ability to avoid peak congestion times was seen as one of the key drivers in requesting an extension of core working hours from 7am to 7pm.

Closely related to recommendations around flexi-time is the request for greater flexibility in general in how, and where, employees work. Increases in technology have opened up tremendous possibilities for organisations to challenge the way in which they work. The rise of tele-working and the popularity of home-working are likely to continue to increase. While these forms of atypical working are not without associated challenges, it is clear that employees appreciate the opportunity to work part of their week from home, or an alternative place of their choosing, which would not require them to present themselves physically at their traditional place of employment. Organisations need to consider fully the implications of embracing tele-working or home-working, both from an employee perspective and an organisational control perspective.

Private sector employees pointed to their desire to introduce, or continue to operate, a compressed working week. The possibility of working slightly longer days, in order to avail of greater flexibility in terms of the actual number of days they work, appears to be an attractive, cost-neutral proposition from both an employee and employer perspective. The notion of a compressed working week is not a new one, although it tends to be more popular in the private sector than the public sector. Where it is in place, it tends to work well. However, organisations need to be careful in planning such an initiative to take full consideration of the legal implications of working longer hours.

While average working hours are falling across the EU, there is no escaping the fact that work is being carried out at a faster pace.[72] The intensification of work has impacted all jobs at all levels and is likely to be the result of changes in the structure of work itself and increased competitive pressures being passed onto workers.[73] It is clear from the findings of the *2007 Work-Life Balance in Ireland* study that those who participated in the study feel this increased pressure and are looking to organisations to provide greater staff resources in order to alleviate these pressures. Employees in both the public and private sector identified increases in staff resources as an area that would have a positive impact on their ability to balance the demands of their work and non-working lives more successfully.

In addition, for the majority of workers, childcare is an area of financial and personal difficulty. Until such time as the government moves to address the issue of childcare to support workers in engaging fully in the economy, this problem is likely to persist. It is unfortunate that organisations are being required to intervene while this vacuum persists. However, organisations that offer on-site childcare facilities, or subsidies towards crèche fees, can benefit from greater employee loyalty and are likely to attract and retain high-performing employees.

Employees increasingly are making employment decisions based on employer attitudes to work-life balance initiatives. These expectations are evident, not only at the recruitment stage but, increasingly, throughout the entire employee career-cycle. These expectations are no longer the sole preserve of female employees, as has traditionally been the case, but employees at different life stages are becoming more vocal about their expectations and needs in relation to work-life balance. The issue of access in terms of the criteria around which certain work-life balance initiatives are made available to different categories of employees is likely to increase over the coming years. Indeed, the need to increase the access employees have to work-life balance initiatives and programmes was highlighted by those in private sector as one of the areas for improvement. Public sector employees who responded to the survey highlighted their desire to have term-time working or a similar programme available and accessible to all employees, irrespective of whether they have childcare responsibilities.

The issue of access is closely matched to the need for senior management to embrace fully the concept of work-life balance and the various initiatives and programmes contained therein. The employees who participated in the *2007 Work Life Balance in Ireland* study cited support, particularly at a senior managerial level, as an area where there is scope for improvement. We know from research that the attitude of management towards work-life balance initiatives has a direct impact on the utilisation or uptake of such policies and initiatives[74] and, indeed, a supportive workplace has been identified as being critical to the successful implementation and uptake of family-friendly policies in particular.[75]

---

[72] Boisard *et al.* (2003).
[73] Green (2004).
[74] Allen (2001).
[75] Thompson *et al.* (1999).

Looking to the Future: Legislative & Policy Developments

This section examines future legislative and policy developments likely to affect WLB programmes both in Ireland and at EU level.

The main EU driver of work-life balance initiatives is the 'Lisbon strategy'.[76] Ratified in 2005, this agreement aims to make the EU "the most competitive and dynamic knowledge-based economy in the world, capable of sustainable economic growth, with more and better jobs and greater social cohesion" by 2010. It also offers a framework for upgrading family policies by encouraging equal opportunities, in particular a better integration of working and family life. During 2008, the interim review of the implementation of the renewed Lisbon strategy will take place. New guidelines for employment will be prepared and existing policies will be improved upon. It is thought that interest groups will lobby for the co-ordination of social security systems for migrant workers, which includes family benefits, to be incorporated into this framework. This is particularly significant in the Irish case, given the large influx of European migrant workers. Furthermore, the recent enlargement of the EU has lead to increased diversity among member states, especially in relation to quality of life. This has resulted in greater demands being put on the limited funds that the EU redistributes to promote social cohesion, including family-friendly policies.

A key political factor influencing WLB policy development is the EU's commitment to expanding the EU labour market by encouraging greater female participation and to reverse the decline in fertility and birth rates. This is evident from the targets laid down by the Barcelona European Council (by 2010, 90% of children aged between three years of age and the mandatory school age must have childcare services available to them).

In a similar vein, the concept of 'flexicurity' is gaining increasing currency at an EU employment policy level. Flexicurity is a new, innovative way of viewing flexibility and security in the labour market. It takes into account the fact that globalisation and technological progress are rapidly changing the needs of workers and enterprises. Organisations increasingly are under pressure to adapt and develop their products and services more quickly. To survive in the current marketplace, companies have to adapt their production methods and their workforce continuously. Encouraging flexible labour markets and maintaining high levels of security will be effective only if employees are given the opportunity to adapt to change and make progress in their working life. Therefore, the flexicurity model places an emphasis on supporting equal opportunities for all and equity between men and women.

The EU policy approach to work-life balance issues is traditionally aimed at measures and policies dealing with particular life phases (for example, the effects of parental leave on work-life balance when children are young). However, life-course policies are beginning to gain in importance at an EU policy level. This will have implications for future WLB initiatives, such as career breaks during later adulthood to engage in life-long learning.

At national level, the Department of Enterprise, Trade & Employment identifies its mission as "working for Government and the people to equitably grow Ireland's competitiveness and quality employment".[77] The National Workplace Strategy, launched by the Taoiseach in 2005, is the Government's blueprint to help transform Irish workplaces into 'workplaces of the future'. The National Workplace Strategy is focused on stimulating workplace change and innovation across five strategic priority areas:

- Commitment to workplace innovation.

---

[76] *Commission of the European Communities* (2005: 981).

[77] www.entemp.ie.

- Capacity for change.
- Developing future skills.
- Access to opportunities.
- Quality of working life.

Moreover, the most recent 10-year framework for social partnership, *Towards 2016*, places WLB as a key priority to ensure Ireland's continued economic development. To achieve this, the work of the National Framework Committee for Work-Life Balance Policies[78] will continue. The Committee is charged with facilitating the development of work-life balance policies at the level of the enterprise through the development of a package of practical measures. Examples of such policies include: flexi-time; part-time working; annualised hours; tele-working; term-time working; work-sharing; job-sharing; and other various additional leave options either paid or unpaid.

A grant support scheme, funded by the Government and implemented by the Equality Authority on behalf of the National Framework Committee for Work-Life Balance, was set up in 2007. The purpose of the scheme is to assist small and medium-sized enterprises in developing, implementing, and evaluating work-life balance policies and arrangements, using a planned and systematic approach. Under the initiative, up to five days' consultancy can be sought and, if approved, will be provided by an experienced consultant who has been appointed to the WLB Consultants Panel.

The Government's attempts to deal with pressing childcare issues is encapsulated in the National Childcare Strategy 2006-2010[79] and the creation of the new Office of the Minister for Children, with a Ministerial seat at the Cabinet table, representing the interests of children and young people. For the first time, this Office brings together the Government Departments of Health & Children, Justice, Equality & Law Reform, and Education & Science, all of which have an input into childcare policy. One of the key elements of the new National Childcare Strategy is the National Childcare Investment Programme 2006–2010, to which the Government has committed €575 million over the next five years. This should result in the development and delivery of new policies and programmes that will help in the provision of childcare to working parents. The outcomes of this process should lead to changes to WLB programmes dealing with parenthood.

In conclusion, as the landscape for WLB programmes and initiatives continues to evolve and develop, organisations will need to respond to changes and developments at a policy level, as well as to changing employee needs and demands. The onus is on both employers and employees to work together to establish, develop and implement work-life balance initiatives that benefit the individual employee and the organisation. The workplace of the future will benefit greatly from a focus on work-life balance and this best practice management guide will assist managers and organisations to provide effective work-life balance solutions. Well-developed, effective and successful WLB practices and procedures will improve the quality of working life, which has positive consequences for employees, organisations, and society in general.

---

[78]   See http://www.worklifebalance.ie and http://www.equality.ie.
[79]   Office for the Ministry of Children (2006).

Chapter Summary

The Future of HR in Europe[80] reports that managing work-life balance is ranked among the top three challenges facing HR through to 2015, according to the HR executives surveyed.

The following recommendations are presented in the report on how HR professionals can address the work-life balance challenge:

- Identify areas for improvement and priorities, by using employee surveys and assessments to identify the options employees' desire for work-life balance.

- Develop key performance indicators to measure work-life balance and its influence on business.

- Assess systematically the current portfolio of work-life balance offerings and make necessary adjustments to ensure they are effective.

- Communicate work-life balance policies, programmes, and offerings to all employees frequently.

- Development of pilot programmes to meet work-life needs.

- Train line managers in work-life balance initiatives and ensure they are incorporated into their business functioning.

The WLB model presented in this book (see **Figure 1.1** and **Chapters 3** to **5**) sets out a process that organisations can follow to address the issues set out above.

This book will act as a useful tool for managers and organisations in the design, implementation, and evaluation of WLB policies and programmes.

The case studies presented in the book provide useful insights into the actual WLB experiences of managers and employees in various organisations in Ireland.

As the evidence presented in this book demonstrates, it will be important for organisations to embrace work-life balance initiatives more fully to enable them to realise the benefits that can be accrued from managing employees' work-life balance effectively.

Understandably, work-life balance policy and practice is not without criticism and there are many challenges to be overcome. Some of these criticisms and challenges have been explored in this book and organisations need to be cognisant of these issues to ensure successful WLB practices.

---

[80] Boston Consulting Group and the European Association of Personnel Managers (2007).

APPENDIX A:
SAMPLE WORK-LIFE BALANCE POLICY

Section	Contents	Page
1	Policy statement	
2	Objectives of the policy	
3	Scope of the policy	
4	Scope of requests for WLB initiatives	
5	Consideration of requests for WLB initiatives	
6	Procedure for requesting WLB initiatives	
7	Reasons for refusing requests for WLB initiatives	
8	Extending timescales	
9	Monitoring and evaluating the policy	
Form 1	WLB Initiative application and confirmation of receipt of request	
Form 2	WLB Initiative application – grant request	
Form 3	WLB Initiative application – refusal	
Form 4	WLB Initiative application - appeal decision	

1.0 Policy Statement

1.1 [Organisation Name] is committed to the principle of work-life balance (WLB) and work-life balance initiatives. [Organisation Name] recognises that there is potential for mutual benefits to the organisation and its employees if WLB initiatives can be successfully implemented and managed. WLB refers to a range of initiatives / flexible working arrangements that go beyond employees' statutory leave entitlements, aimed at helping them balance their work and personal lives.

1.2 The organisation acknowledges that individuals work best when they can balance their work responsibilities with their personal / non-work life. As a result every reasonable effort will be made to try to accommodate WLB initiatives, as well as continuing to meet the business needs of the organisation.

2.0 Objectives of the Policy

2.1 The key objectives of the policy are:

2.1.1 To support [Organisation Name]'s commitment to the principle of ensuring that employees can attain balance in their work and non-work life.

2.1.2 To facilitate the retention of experienced and valuable skilled employees.

2.1.3 To improve staff morale and maintains high levels of employee commitment and performance.

2.1.4 To increase [organisation name] competitiveness in the recruitment market, attracting quality applicants for vacancies from a wider audience.

2.1.5 To ensure that [organisation name] retains productivity levels to meet its business needs and objectives and maintain a competitive advantage in the marketplace.

2.1.6 To ensure that [organisation name] meets its statutory obligations required by Irish legislation.

2.2 Taking account of these objectives, the policy has been developed in line with best practice and supports the organisation's strategic priority of becoming an "Employer of Choice".

3.0 Scope of the Policy

3.1 The organisation will endeavour to meet employee needs under the statutory leave entitlements.

3.2 However,[organisation name] recognises that WLB initiatives/flexible working beyond those statutory entitlements may be required by employees at various stages in their working life. Therefore, this policy is not just limited to working parents and carers - instead all staff who have a minimum of [specify service e.g. 26 weeks up to two years] continuous service fall within the scope of this policy.

3.3 The policy has been developed to assist [organisation name] commitment to supporting its employees to combine their work with their family life, caring responsibilities and with their personal life outside of the workplace.

3.4 The policy sets out a planned and systematic approach to managing WLB initiatives which will enable all employee WLB requests to be dealt with, in a clear, consistent and fair manner.

4.0 Scope of Requests

4.1 Examples of requests to avail of WLB initiatives may include:
4.1.1 Part-time – reduced working hours
4.1.2 Job-sharing or Work-sharing
4.1.3 Term-time working – taking time off during school holidays to support childcare (only available to working parents with school-going children)
4.1.4 Life-Balance Time – which can be used by employees to facilitate a range of needs, including personal development, education, travel, childcare, time out and preparing for retirement.
4.1.5 Flexi-time – flexibility in start/finish times and working within specified core hours
4.1.6 Education schemes – where employees can obtain financial support/time off to pursue further education
4.1.7 Career breaks – where employees can opt to take time out from work, which can range between 6 months to 5 years.

5.0 Consideration of requests

5.1 The following criteria for eligibility will be considered when a request to avail of a WLB initiative is made by an employee.
5.1.1 **Operational considerations:** All requests will be considered by the appropriate Middle/Line Manager who must take into account the specific circumstances of our operational environment. In particular, any decision to accommodate a particular request to avail of WLB initiatives, must consider the core operational needs of the business priorities.
5.1.2 **Length of Service within the organisation**: Employees must have [typically 26 weeks – 2 years] service to be considered to avail of WLB initiatives
5.1.3 **Flexibility and timing of the request**: i.e. is it suitable for the work schedules and business needs at that time.
5.1.4 **Is the employee already availing of another WLB initiative**: For example, if an employee is availing of job-sharing, s/he will be unable to avail of term-time or life-balance time or any other WLB initiative at that time.
5.1.5 **Has an employee availed of a WLB initiative in the previous 12 months**: If so, they may not be considered again immediately.

5.2 Wherever possible, middle / line managers will try to reach a decision within [for example 6 weeks] after receiving the request. However, it is important to note that consideration of a request may take longer, particularly if there are certain operational difficulties, which need to be overcome.

5.3 Managers and individuals should be aware that if a decision is made to accommodate a particular request, then this change can be permanent, temporary or on a trial basis. This can vary depending on the organisational business priorities and needs. Additionally, it must be noted that changes in business demands may require a review of the agreed change in the working pattern.

6.0 Procedure for Requesting WLB initiatives

6.1 When an employee makes a request to avail of a WLB initiative, they must meet the criteria as set out in 5.1.

6.2 An application to request availing of a WLB initiative using [Form 1: WLB Initiative Application] should be completed and submitted to the middle / line Manager. The employee should allow sufficient time for the request to be considered.

6.3 Written confirmation of the receipt of the application using [Form 1: WLB Initiative Application] should be sent to the individual, within one week. A copy of the request should also be sent to the HR function for entry onto the 'WLB Initiative Request Register' on the HR database.

6.4 Prior to discussing their request with the manager, the employee must consider the issues which may impact upon their application to avail of the WLB initiative. In particular, they should consider how their request to avail of the WLB initiative will impact on their job role, potential challenges in terms of their own work, if their request is granted and how that will impact on their colleagues.

6.5 The middle / line manager should consider the request for the WLB initiative by taking into account the specific circumstances of the business needs/environment. In particular, any decision to accommodate a particular request for a WLB initiative should consider the core operational needs relating to the business needs and the employee needs. In addition, the manager must consider the reasons the employee has made the request and if the type of change requested is permanent or temporary and the proposed date for implementation.

6.6 The manager should then arrange a meeting with the employee within [specify time, e.g. 3 weeks] of receiving the application.

6.7 Prior to this meeting, the manager will conduct an initial assessment of the request based on the details submitted on the application form. This will involve liaising with the relevant stakeholders e.g. individuals who are involved in the co-ordination and planning of business needs, before any decisions on the feasibility of the request are made.

6.8 On meeting the employee, the impact of availing of the WLB initiative on both the business performance together with the impact on existing staff should be discussed in detail. If following the initial assessment, it appears that the request from the employee to avail of the WLB initiative cannot be accommodated, these issues must be discussed with the employee at that meeting and alternative options explored with them.

6.9 Middle / line managers should consult with the HR Function, where it appears that the request cannot be accommodated. If appropriate, a HR representative will also attend the meeting to help facilitate a discussion around alternatives and reach a compromise.

6.10 If an employee applies for a temporary change to their working pattern, this may be agreed upon up to a maximum of [e.g. 6 months]. Employees accepting a temporary change will automatically revert back to their original working pattern at the end of the temporary agreement, but may not revert back to their previous job role, if a change of job role was necessary to accommodate their request to avail of the WLB initiative

6.11 If an employee is granted a request to avail of a WLB initiative on a trial basis, this can be for a short period of time [1-3 months]. A change on a trial basis can apply when the middle / line manager is unsure of the impact that granting the request to avail of the WLB initiative will have on the business needs. The trial period will allow the manager to test if the new working arrangement is practical and feasible. Employees accepting a trial basis change will automatically revert back to their original working pattern at the end of the agreement, unless a new agreement is reached.

6.12 When an employee is granted a request to avail of a WLB initiative on a permanent basis, this will involve a change to the employee's working pattern and their terms and conditions in their contract of employment. When a change is permanent, there will be no automatic right for the employee to revert back to their previous working pattern or their previous job role, if a change of job role was necessary to accommodate their request to avail of the WLB initiative.

6.13 Following the meeting with the employee, the manager must notify the employee of the decision in writing within [specify period of time e.g. 3 weeks] of the date of the meeting using [Form 2: WLB Initiative Application: Grant Request] This notification will:

6.13.1 Accept the request and establish a start date

6.13.2 Confirm if the agreement to grant the change is for a permanent, temporary or trial basis.

6.13.3 Form 2 should be forwarded to the HR function to allow details to be entered onto the WLB Initiative Request Register and filed on the personnel file.

6.14 If the decision is made to refuse the request, the manager must notify the employee within [specify period of time e.g. 3 weeks] of the date of the meeting using [Form 3: WLB Initiative Application: Refuse Request]. This notification will:

6.14.1 Refuse the request, setting out clearly the reasons for the refusal together with notification of the appeals process.

6.14.2 A copy of Form 3 should be forwarded to the HR Function to allow details to be entered onto the WLB Initiative Request Register on the HR database.

6.15 Employees wishing to appeal the decision not to grant their request to avail of a WLB initiative should do so within [specify period of time e.g. 2 weeks] using [Form 4: WLB Initiative Application: Appeal Decision]. This form should be completed and forwarded to the appropriate middle / line manager, who originally made the decision to refuse the request.

6.16 The middle / line manager must then date the form to indicate when they received it and immediately inform their Senior Manager and HR Function of the appeal and forward all relevant documentation relating to the application.

6.17 The middle / line manager should arrange a further meeting with the employee within [specify period of time, e.g. 2 weeks] of receiving the application to appeal. The employee should be informed that they can be accompanied by a staff colleague/employee representative. A representative from the HR function should also attend the meeting.

6.18 Within [specify period of time e.g. 2 weeks] after this meeting, the manager must notify the employee in writing of the decision on the appeal. The notification will either:

6.18.1 Support the appeal and specify the agreed change in the working pattern, together with details of the start date using [Form 2: WLB Initiative Application: Grant Request] or

6.18.2 Dismiss the appeal, stating clearly the grounds for the decision and providing an explanation of the refusal using [Form 3: WLB Initiative Application: Refuse Request]

6.19 The decision made on appeal is final. A copy of the decision should be forwarded to the HR function to allow the details to be entered onto the WLB Initiative Request Register on the HR database.

7.0 Reasons for Refusing Requests for WLB initiatives

7.1 Requests to avail of WLB initiatives can only be refused for one or more of the following reasons:

7.1.1 The damaging impact on the performance of the organisation, the ability to meet customer requirements or the quality of work or service to the customers.

7.1.2 Inability to re-organise work among existing employees

7.1.3 Unable to recruit additional staff to cover the change in the working pattern.

7.1.4 The burden of additional costs.

7.1.5 Insufficient demand for work during the period when an employee proposes to work.

8.0 Extending Timescales

8.1 The timescales for granting requests i.e. period of change, permanent, temporary or trial basis, as set out above should be adhered to by all managers. However, if a manager and an employee mutually agree to extend any of the time limits, this agreement should be recorded in writing and must specify the period to which the extension relates and the date on which the extension is to end. A copy of this written record must be provided to the individual and a copy placed on their personnel file.

9.0 Monitoring & Evaluation of the policy

9.1 An annual review of this policy will be undertaken jointly between management representatives and employee representatives. Ongoing evaluation will also take place, using various methods to assess and evaluate the contribution of the WLB initiatives from an organisational and individual perspective. Both quantitative and qualitative data can be gathered from the WLB Initiative request register on the HR database, from employee satisfaction surveys, focus groups, one-to-one feedback between managers and employees, and performance appraisals.

Source: Adapted from East Midlands Ambulance Service NHS Trust (2007) and West Hertfordshire Hospitals NHS Trust (2005).

APPENDIX B:
SAMPLE FORMS FOR IMPLEMENTATION
OF WLB INITIATIVES

Form 1: WLB Initiative Application

Form 2: WLB Initiative Application – Grant Request

Form 3: WLB Initiative Application – Refuse Request

Form 4: WLB Initiative Application – Appeal Decision

Form 1: WLB Initiative Application

Note to the Employee

This is the official form to be completed when applying to avail of a WLB initiative. It is important that you complete all sections. It will help your Manager to make a decision if you can give detailed information where possible with regard to the initiative you wish to avail of e.g. flexible working, term-time or life-balance time, etc.

Please note that a certain set of criteria apply to any application to avail of WLB initiatives including:

- *Operational issues (i.e. business needs versus the employee needs)*
- *Length of service (specify period of time, e.g. 26 weeks – 2 years)*
- *Flexibility of timing of the request (e.g. is it suitable for work patterns and business needs at that time)*
- *Is the employee availing of another WLB initiative*
- *Has the employee availed of a WLB initiative in the past 12 months*

When you have completed this form, please give it to your immediate Supervisor/Manager. Your Supervisor/Manager will arrange a meeting with you within the next _____ to discuss in greater detail your request in order to make a decision.

Please note that wherever possible it would be the intention of the Supervisor/Manager to make a decision on your request within [*Specify period of time, e.g. 6 weeks*] of the original request. However, consideration of some requests may take longer where difficulties may need to be overcome. Therefore, it is important that you make your application to avail of a WLB initiative well in advance of the date you wish the request to take effect.

In your application, you will be requested to describe how you think the new working pattern will impact on the service/support function in which your work and how it will impact on your colleagues. In addition, you are asked to describe how you think that the impact on both areas can be dealt with.

If your request is granted, you will be informed in writing on *"Form 2: WLB Initiative Application – Grant Request"*. If a permanent change to your working pattern is agreed, please note that this will represent a permanent change to your terms and conditions of employment. However, a temporary arrangement of up to _____ can be agreed or a trial period of _____ may be allowed, if your manager is unsure that the arrangement will work. A period of review on all agreed working patterns will apply.

If a decision is made not to grant your request, you will be informed in writing by your middle / line manager on *Form 3: WLB Initiative Application – Refuse Request*, stating the reasons why. In this event, you have the right to appeal the decision using *"Form 4: WLB Initiative Application: Appeal Decision"*

1. Personal Details:

Name of Applicant: _____ Payroll/ Staff Number: _____

Job Title:_____
Department:_____

Reporting
to:_____

Date commenced employment [_____]

2. Reasons for making the request:

I wish to apply to make a **Temporary** ☐ **Permanent** ☐ change to my working pattern for the following reason(s):

> **Childcare**
> **Eldercare**
> **Need/Want more personal time**
> **Term-time/Life Balance time**
> **Education**
> **Career break**
> **Other (please detail below)**

3. Current working pattern

4. Desired Working Pattern

Please outline clearly below the working pattern you require to work:

Please state when you require this working pattern to commence from:

5. Impact of new Working Pattern:

Describe how you think this change in your working pattern will affect the operational service / support function in which you work and how you think it will affect your colleagues.

Impact on the service / support function:

Impact on your colleagues:

6. Accommodating the New Working Pattern:

6.a Please describe how you think that the effect on the service/support function can be dealt with?

6.b Please describe how you think the effect on your colleagues can be dealt with?

6. Declaration

I declare that I have not made an application for a WLB initiative in the past twelve months and I confirm that I have _____ weeks / years with this organisation.

Signed: *Employee*
Date:

Please detach and return to employee

--- **cut here**

Manager's Confirmation of Receipt of Flexible Working Application

Dear

I confirm that I have received your request to change your work pattern on ....(date)

Following consideration of your request for flexible working, I shall be arranging a meeting to discuss your request within _____ weeks from this date.

Signed: *Middle / line manager*
Date:

Form 2: WLB Initiative Application: Grant Request

Note to employer

You must write to your employee within _____ days following the meeting conveying your decision. This form should be completed by the employer when accepting an application to avail of a WLB initiative. If you cannot accommodate the requested working pattern, you may still wish to explore alternatives to find a working pattern suitable to both of you.

Please note that **Form 3: WLB Initiative Application: Refuse Request** should be used if you are unable to accommodate the employee's request and no other alternatives can be found.

Note to the employee

We are pleased to inform you that your request to avail of a WLB initiative has been accepted. The change in your working pattern is described as [e.g. Reduced Working Hours or Job-Sharing or Flexi-time] which will be:

Permanent ☐

Temporary Period
[specify period of time] ☐

Trial Period
[specify period of time] ☐

and will commence on: (date)

Due to this change in your working pattern, it is important that you consider the following details:

	Details	Specify Change (if applicable)
1	Job Role – changed [Permanent or Temporary]	
2	Contract of Employment – changed [Permanent or Temporary]	
3	Remuneration [Reduced on pro-rata basis for hours worked or unpaid leave]	
4	Annual Leave/Public Holidays	
5	Pension/Superannuation [un-paid leave does not count for superannuation purposes]	
6	Date of Return to original working pattern [Temporary or Trial Period]	
7	Extension of Time [Option]	
8	Review Period	

Signed:

Middle / line manager	*Date:*
HR Representative	*Date:*
Employee	*Date:*

Form 3: WLB Initiative Application: Refuse Request

Note to Employer

Following a meeting with your employee, and full and careful consideration of the employee request to avail of a WLB initiative, and you find that you are unable to accommodate their request, you must write to your employee within _____ days. You must state the reasons [e.g. business grounds] as to why you are unable to accommodate their request at this time. The list of the permissible business grounds under which a request may be refused are detailed in the Work-Life Balance Sample Policy (Appendix A).

Reasons why your flexible working application has been rejected

Dear ……………….

Following receipt of your WLB initiative application and our subsequent meeting on …………. we regret that we are unable to accommodate your request for the following reason(s):

1.
2.
3.

We have considered the other work pattern(s) we discussed at our meeting and also find that they are not suitable at this time for the following reason(s):

1.
2.
3.

If you are unhappy with the decision you may appeal against it, using **Form 4: WLB Initiative Application: Appeal Decision**

Signed:

Middle / line manager	**Date:**
HR Representative	**Date:**

Form 4: WLB Initiative Application: Appeal Decision

Note to the Employee:

If your application to avail of a WLB initiative has been refused by your employer, you have the right to appeal this decision. You should use this form to make your appeal. You should set out your grounds for appealing and do so within 2 weeks of receiving written notice that your application has been refused.

Note to the Employer:

This is a formal appeal to your decision to refuse the employee to avail of a WLB initiative. You have 2 weeks to arrange a formal meeting with the employee to discuss your reasons for not granting their request at this time

Dear

I wish to appeal against your decision to refuse my application for flexible working. I am appealing on the following ground(s):

1.
2.
3.

Additional Information to support your appeal

Signed:	*Employee*
Date:	

Source: Adapted from East Midlands Ambulance Service NHS Trust (2007) and West Hertfordshire Hospitals NHS Trust (2005).

Bibliography

Allen, T.D. (2001). 'Family-supportive work environments: The role of organisational perceptions', *Journal of Vocational Behaviour* 58(3): 414-435.

Anderson, V. (2007). The Value of Learning – *A New Model of Value & Evaluation*, London: Chartered Institute of Personnel & Development.

Backhaus, K. & Tikoo, S. (2004). 'Conceptualizing and researching employer brands', *Career Development International* 9(5): 501-517.

Barney, J. (1991). 'Firm resources and sustained competitive advantage', *Journal of Management* 17: 99-120.

Belshaw, K. (2004). *Joe Burnout*, Dublin: VHI, available at http://www.vhi.ie/hfiles/hf-194.jsp accessed 21 March 2008.

Bingham, C. & Cuff, P. (2002). *Internal Communication*, Managing Best Practice No.100, London: Work Foundation.

Bodin, R.P. & Verborgh, E. (2002). *Quality of Work & Employment in Europe: Issues & Challenges*, Dublin: European Foundation for the Improvement of Living and Working Conditions.

Boisard, P., Cartron, D., Gollac, M., Valeyre, A. & Besancon, J.B. (2003). *Time & Work: Work Intensity*, Dublin: European Foundation for the Improvement of Living & Working Conditions.

Boston Consulting Group and European Association for Personnel Management (2007). *The Future of HR in Europe: Key Challenges through 2015*, Boston: Boston Consulting Group.

Bowman, M., Carlson, P.M., Colvin, R.E. & Green, G.E. (2006). 'The loss of talent', *Public Personnel Management* 35(2): 121-136.

Chartered Institute of Personnel & Development (2003). *Living to Work? Survey Report*, London: Chartered Institute of Personnel & Development.

Chartered Institute of Personnel & Development (2005). *Evaluation & Value Model* [online], available at http://www.cipd.co.uk/subjects/lrnanddev/evaluation/_vlrngnwmdl.htm, accessed 10 November 2007.

Chartered Institute of Personnel & Development (2006a). *How Engaged are British Employees? Survey Report 2006* [online] available at http://www.cipd.co.uk/onlineinfodocuments/ atozresources.htm, accessed 12 November 2007.

Chartered Institute of Personnel & Development (2006b). *Flexible Working: Roles & Responsibilities* [online], available at http://www.cipd.co.uk/onlineinfodocuments/ atozresources.htm, accessed on 10 November 2007.

Chartered Institute of Personnel & Development (2006c). *Learning & Development: Annual Survey Report 2006* [online], available at http://www.cipd.co.uk/onlineinfodocuments/ atozresources.htm, accessed 10 December 2007.

Chartered Institute of Personnel & Development (2007a). *Work-Life Balance Fact-Sheet*, available at http://www.cipd.co.uk/subjects/wrkgtime/wrktmewrklfbal/worklifeba.htm.

Chartered Institute of Personnel & Development (2007b). *Employee Communication* [online], available at http://www.cipd.co.uk/onlineinfodocuments/ atozresources.htm , accessed on 10 November 2007.

Chartered Institute of Personnel & Development (2007c). *Helping People Learn: Overview & Update* [online], available at http://www.cipd.co.uk/helpingpeoplelearn, accessed on 14 December 2007.

Chartered Institute of Personnel & Development (2007d). *Change Agenda: The Value of Learning – A New Model of Value & Evaluation* [online], available at http://www.cipd.co.uk/onlineinfodocuments/atozresources.htm, accessed 10 December 2007.

Chartered Institute of Personnel & Development (2007e). 'The power of brand', *IMPACT: Quarterly Update on CIPD Policy & Research* 21, November.

Christensen, P.M. (1999). 'Toward a comprehensive work / life strategy', in Parasuraman, S. & Greenhaus, J.H. (eds.). *Integrating Work & Family: Challenges & Choices for a Changing World*, Westport, CT: Praeger.

CIPD – *see* Chartered Institute of Personnel & Development.

Commission of the European Communities (2005). *Common Actions for Growth & Employment: The Community Lisbon Programme*, Brussels: Commission of the European Communities.

Department of An Taoiseach (2000). *Programme for Prosperity & Fairness*, Dublin: Government Stationery Office.

Department of An Taoiseach (2006). *Towards 2016 - Ten-Year Framework Social Partnership Agreement 2006-2015*, Dublin: Government Stationery Office.

Department of Justice, Equality & Law Reform (2005). *Employees (Provision of Information & Consultation Act 2005,* Dublin: Government Stationery Office.

Department of Labour (New Zealand) (2006). *Work-Life Balance: Making It Work for Your Business* [online] available at http://www.dol.govt.nz/worklife/index.asp, accessed on 29 November 2007.

Duggan, D., Hughes, G. & Sexton, J. (1997). *Occupational Employment Forecasts 2003*, FÁS / ESRI Manpower Forecasting Studies, Report 6, November, Dublin: FÁS / Economic & Social Research Institute.

East Midlands Ambulance Service NHS Trust (2007). *Work-Life Balance Policy* [online], available at http://www.emas.nhs.uk/EasysiteWeb/getresource.axd?AssetID=3889 &type=Full&servicetype=Attachment, accessed 5 November 2007.

Edwards, J.E., Scott, J.C., & Raju, N.S. (2003). *The Human Resources Program – Evaluation Handbook*, Thousand Oaks, CA: Sage.

Eisenberger, R., Stinglhamber, F.,Vandenberghe, C., Sucharski, I. & Rhoades, L. (2002). 'Perceived supervisor support: Contributions to perceived Organisational support and employee retention', *Journal of Applied Psychology* 87(3): 565-573.

European Foundation for the Improvement of Living & Working Conditions (2002). *Quality of Work & Employment in Europe: Issues & Challenges*, Foundation Paper No.1, Dublin: European Foundation for the Improvement of Living & Working Conditions.

Fine-Davis, M. & Clarke, H. (2002). 'Better childcare and public transport seen as vital for work-life balance', *Work-Life Balance Conference,* Trinity College Dublin.

Forret, M. & de Jansaz, S. (2005). Perceptions of an organization's culture for work and family: Do mentors make a difference?', *Career Development International*, 10(6/7): 478-492.

Fried, M. (1999). *Evaluation Using a Participatory Approach in Metrics Manual: Ten Approaches to Measuring Work / Life*, Boston MA: Boston College Center for Work & Family.

George, J.M. & Jones, G.R. (2007). *Understanding & Managing Organisational Behaviour*, fourth edition, London: Pearson Publishing.

Gratton, L. (2003). 'The Humpty Dumpty effect', *People Management* 9(9), 11 May.

Green, F. (2004). 'Why has work effort become more intense?', *Industrial Relations* 43(4).

Greenhaus, J.H. & Powell, G.N. (2006). 'When work and family are allies: A theory of work-family enrichment', *Academy of Management Review* 31(1): 72-92.

Guest, D. (2001). 'Perspectives on the study of work-life balance', European Network of Organisational Psychology Symposium, Paris.

HRSDC – see Human Resource & Social Development Canada.

Hudson Highland Group (2005). *The Case for Work / Life Balance: Closing the Gap between Policy & Practice*, Sydney: Hudson Highland Group.

Hughes, J. & Bozionelos, N. (2007). 'Work-life balance as source of job dissatisfaction and withdrawal attitudes: An exploratory study on the views of male workers', *Personnel Review* 36(1): 145-154.

Human Resource & Social Development Canada (2005). *The Work-Life Continuum (Assessment & Planning)*, available at: http://www.hrsdc.gc.ca/en/lp/spila/wlb/imt /11worklife_continuum.shtml, accessed 1 December 2007.

Johnson, A.A. (1995). 'The business case for work-family programmes', *Journal of Accountancy* 180(2): 53-8.

Joshi, S., Leichne, J., Melanson, K., Pruna, C., Sager, N., Story, C.J. & Williams, K. (2002). *Work-Life Balance …: A case of Social Responsibility or Competitive Advantage?*, Atlanta: Georgia Institute of Technology.

Kossek, E.E., Barber, A. & Winters, D. (1999). 'Using flexible schedules in the managerial world: The power of peers', *Human Resource Management* 38: 33–46.

Labour Relations Commission (2006). *Code of Practice on Access to Part-Time Work*, Dublin: Government Stationery Office.

Litz, R.A. & Stewart, A.C. (2000). 'Trade name franchise membership as a human resource management strategy: Does buying group training deliver true value for small retailers?', *Entrepreneurship Theory & Practice* 25(1).

LRC – see Labour Relations Commission.

McCarthy, A., Grady, G. & Darcy, C. (2007). 'Work-life balance in organisations: Investigating the role of the line manager', paper presented at the 9th International Human Resource Management Conference, Tallinn, June.

McCarthy, A., Grady, G., Darcy, C. & Kirrane, M. (2008). *Work-Life Balance 2007: Research Report*, available at http://www.nuigalway.ie/management/staff/mccarthy/index.htm.

McCauley, C. & Wakefield, M. (2006). 'Talent management in the 21st century', *The Journal for Quality & Participation*, Winter, 4-7.

McConville, T. & Holden, L. (1999). 'The filling in the sandwich: HRM and middle managers in the health sector', *Personnel Review*, 28 (5&6): 406-424.

Nord, W.R., Fox, S., Phoenix, A. & Viano, K. (2002). 'Real world reactions to work-life balance programs: Lessons for effective implementation', *Organizational Dynamics* 30(3): 223-238.

O'Connell, P.J., Russell, R., Williams, J & Blackwell, S. (2003). *The Changing Workplace: A Survey of Employees' Views & Experiences*, Dublin: Forum on the Workplace of the Future / National Centre for Partnership & Performance.

Office for the Ministry of Children. (2006). *National Childcare Strategy: A Guide for Parents*, Dublin: Department of Health & Children.

Parasuraman, S. & Greenhaus, J.H. (1999). *Integrating Work & Family: Challenges & Choices for a Changing World*, Westport, CT: Praeger.

Poelmans, S. & Sahibzada, K. (2004). 'A multi-level model for studying the context and impact of work-family policies and culture in organisations', *Human Resource Management Review* 14: 409-431.

Poelmans, S.A.Y., Chinchilla, N. & Cardona, P. (2003). 'The adoption of family-friendly HRM policies', *International Journal of Manpower* 24(2): 128-147.

Purcell, J. & Hutchinson, S. (2007). 'Front-line managers as agents in the HRM-performance causal chain: Theory, analysis and evidence, *Human Resource Management Journal*, 17(1): 3-20.

QGDoEIR – see Queensland Government Department of Employment & Industrial Relations.

Queensland Government Department of Employment & Industrial Relations (2007). *Work, Family & Lifestyle*, available at http://www.deir.qld.gov.au.

Scandura, T.A. & Lankau, M.J. (1997). 'Relationships of gender, family responsibility and flexible work hours to organizational commitment and job satisfaction', *Journal of Organizational Behaviour* 18(4): 377-391.

Sexton, J.J., Hughes, G. & Finn, C. (2002). *Occupational Employment Forecasts 2015*, Dublin: FÁS / ESRI Manpower Forecasting Studies

Small Firms Association (2005). 5th National Absenteeism Report 2005, Dublin: Small Firms Association.

Sullivan, S.E. & Mainiero, S.E. (2007). 'Kaleidoscope careers: Benchmarking ideas for fostering family-friendly workplaces, *Organizational Dynamics*, 36: 45-62.

Thompson, C.A., Beauvais, L.A. & Lyness, K.S. (1999). 'When work-family benefits are not enough: The influence of work-family culture on benefit utilisation, organisational attachment and work-family conflict', *Journal of Vocational Behaviour* 54(3): 392-415.

West Hertfordshire Hospitals NHS Trust (2005). *Work-Life Balance Policy & Procedure* [online], available at http://www.westhertshospitals.nhs.uk/work_life_policy.pdf, accessed 5 November 2007.

Work-Life Balance Network (2004). *Work-Life Balance Network Diagnostic Pack*, Dublin: Work-Life Balance Network.

World Health Organisation (2001). *World Health Report 2001 – Mental Health: New Understanding*, Geneva: World Health Organisation.

INDEX

OAK TREE PRESS

is Ireland's leading business book publisher.

It develops and delivers
information, advice and resources
to entrepreneurs and managers –
and those who educate and support them.

Its print, software and web materials
are in use in Ireland, the UK, Finland,
Greece, Norway and Slovenia.

OAK TREE PRESS

19 Rutland Street
Cork, Ireland
T: + 353 21 4313855
F: + 353 21 4313496
E: info@oaktreepress.com
W: www.oaktreepress.com